Filmspeak

Filmspeak

How to Understand Literary Theory by Watching Movies

EDWARD L. TOMARKEN

BLOOMSBURY

NEW YORK • LONDON • NEW DELHI • SYDNEY

Bloomsbury Academic

An imprint of Bloomsbury Publishing Plc

175 Fifth Avenue	50 Bedford Square
New York	London
NY 10010	WC1B 3DP
USA	UK

www.bloomsbury.com

First published 2012

© Edward L. Tomarken, 2012

Library of Congress Cataloging-in-Publication Data
A catalog record for this book is available from the Library of Congress.

ISBN: HB: 978-0-8264-2892-9
PB: 978-0-8264-2893-6

Typeset by Fakenham Preprss Solutions, Fakenham, Norfolk NR21 8NN
Printed and bound in the United States of America

In memory of
Peter David Tomarken 1942–2006

To
Beau, Emma, and Jamie Grimes

For
My Literary Theory Students

Deign on the passing World to turn thine Eyes,
And pause awhile from Learning, to be wise
Samuel Johnson: "The Vanity of Human Wishes," 1749, ll. 157–8

CONTENTS

ACKNOWLEDGMENTS

This book would not exist without the inspiration and encouragement of Evander Lomke. Having located the germ of an idea for the book in a Christmas e-mail, he suggested writing up an outline and then eventually issued the contract. Since that point a few years ago, he has always been there, offering encouragement and invaluable advice throughout the composition and revision of the manuscript. David Barker skilfully guided the first version through expansion and extensive revisions. Kim Storry and her staff promptly and carefully prepared the manuscript for publication. My greatest debt, as ever, is to my beloved wife, Annette Tomarken, who throughout the process provided cogent criticism and a keen eye for proof-reading, all during completion of her own scholarly project.

FILMS ANALYZED

Chapter One

"Inglourious Basterds" (2009)
"Kill Bill, Vol. 2" (2004)
"The Dark Knight" (2008)
"The Bourne Supremacy" (2004)
"Everyone Says I Love You" (1996)
"Deconstructing Harry" (1997)
"Man of the Year" (2006)

Chapter Two

"Shakespeare in Love" (1998)
"Slumdog Millionaire" (2008)
"An Education" (2009)
"Bridget Jones's Diary" (2001)
"Bridget Jones: The Edge of Reason" (2004)

Chapter Three

"The Da Vinci Code" (2006)
"Amélie" (2001)
"Run Lola Run" (1998)
"A Single Man" (2008)
"The Godfather: Part III" (1990)
"Vicki Cristina Barcelona" (2008)

Chapter Four

Chapter Five

Chapter Six

INTRODUCTION

The idea of using contemporary film to teach literary theory came from my students. They complained that the literary theory reading assignments were at best puzzling and at worst incomprehensible. I therefore selected some central ideas in the readings and explained them in less abstruse terms than those of the theorists whose writings were after all intended not for undergraduates but for specialists in the field. Once the light began to dawn, I encouraged the students to return to the written texts and to apply the theories to their problems as budding literary critics. To my surprise, almost without exception the students found illustrations of and uses for these ideas in contemporary movies. On one memorable occasion, a student remarked in the midst of a discussion of the work of Jacques Derrida, "Dr. T., Derrida sucks, you should see 'Kill Bill 2'!" Tarantino's films were known to be very violent, so my wife was horrified when she saw me arrive from the video shop with "Kill Bill 2." But after viewing the film that did indeed strike me as very violent, I came to realize that the student was right; some of Derrida's ideas could be applied to the movie. During discussion of the movie in class it became clear that the students grasped from the film ideas that had eluded them in reading.

Students continued to recommend movies related to the theories discussed in class, and I began to realize that major elements of literary theory could be explained by analysis of certain films. Since many of the films included in this book are adaptations of books, for the most part works of popular fiction, theory pertains to literature as well as movies. This study focuses on movies because students and many members of a general audience are more at ease with films than with texts. Moreover, movies reach a different and probably larger audience than literary theory or even literature.

I stress that the films included here are not artsy forms of cinema, but blockbuster mainstays because they provide the basis for the two goals of this book:

1   to introduce the non-specialist to some basic conceptions of literary theory that relate to concerns of our daily life;

2   to show how the arcane notions of literary theory are entering our culture and can be understood by way of commercially successful movies that speak to all of us.

My object is to show how theory is clarified by film and film is elucidated by theory, not to judge the artistic merit of the films.

The book is comprised of six chapters and a final section of "Suggestions for Teaching Literary Theory." Each chapter is devoted to one theory or theorist in relation to a number of recent films, and the teaching suggestions are divided into portions related to each chapter. My hope is that the reader will be familiar with at least one or two of the films in each chapter. At the outset it is important to make clear that, since I am not an expert on cinema, my analysis of the films will not involve technical language. Film here serves as a tool for teaching and learning. In fact, it soon became clear that my students were more attuned to cinematic techniques than I was. Yet they had little respect for most of these films, believing that box office successes were unlikely to contain important ideas—indeed any ideas at all—except those that improved the ticket sales. So I learned from them what movies to watch, how they responded to them, and was then able to teach them, or so I hope, how theory helps us understand what they enjoyed and learned from the films.

After teaching this class for a second time I began to realize that literary theory—considered one of the most difficult and complex of specialties, involving texts thought by some in the field to be written with deliberate obscurity and intended for a sort of club of exclusive readers—had a particular relevance to popular culture. Yet the biggest problem in teaching beginners is the belief that theory is for a higher order of beings who speak a language that no one else understands. In this respect, the genesis of the contract for this book is of interest. When this class was initiated I had taught for many years at university and published a number of books and essays, all designed for a scholarly and academic audience, not for students or the general reader. But I happened to be in regular e-mail correspondence with a student from an early part of my career who had become a Senior Editor at Continuum International (now owned by Bloomsbury Publishing), the publisher of this book. Evander Lomke, the student from my "green and salad days," was of the generation after me and before my students; his vision was Janus-faced, in between his professor and current students. From his vantage point the book seemed to have—I can only hope that he is right—a significance beyond that of the classroom, to have some interest and potential appeal to a larger audience.

Before beginning, I should make clear that the conception of literary theory presented here is not accepted by all in the field. My view is based upon that of the two professors who first taught me theory, Ralph Cohen and Northrop Frye. Frye's great work, *The Anatomy of Criticism*, (1957), is an application of theory to practical criticism. Frye and Cohen shared the belief that the purpose of theory was for resolving problems of literary analysis. Although at a higher level of generality, theory served as the handmaiden of literary critics. Cohen founded the most important journal in the field, *New Literary History*, in 1969 when literary theory was first recognized as an academic discipline. However, it is important to keep in mind that some view literary theory as a continuation of aesthetics, beginning with Aristotle and Plato. My position, following in the footsteps of Cohen and Frye, applies literary theory to the practical criticism of film. I do not wish to assert that the makers of these films were interested in theory or in using film to exemplify theory. Rather, some contemporary movies help us understand theory, and theory in turn gives us a greater appreciation of cinema. The ideas themselves are embedded in our culture, an element of what used to be called the Zeitgeist, the spirit of the age. The application of a given film to a particular theory should not be seen as precluding the possibility of applying the same film to one of the other theories in this study. In fact, many of the movies are illustrative of a number of the theories, another indication that these ideas are pervading our intellectual environment.

The first question that arises for those who, like myself, do not believe that literary theory is a branch of philosophy is why it became a new field of specialization in the 1960s and 1970s. Literary theory arose in response to the preponderance of formalisms of various kinds in the mid-twentieth century, namely, the assumption that certain themes were inherent or immanent in literature. These views, from structuralism in Europe to New Criticism in the United States and the United Kingdom, were derived from the Russian formalists who came to prominence in the West during the first two decades of the twentieth century. The formalists asserted that the structure or form of art, if properly understood, contained or imparted clear themes. René Wellek and Austin Warren, in *The Theory of Literature* (1946), devised a theory of "norms." Cohen explained this notion of literature as a layer cake; a slice from any side cuts through all of the layers or norms. The point of Wellek and Warren's argument was to assert that whatever the point of view of the reader, norms evoked similar themes. For instance, T. S. Eliot's phrase, "the butt-ends of our days and ways" in "The Love Song of J. Alfred Prufrock" transforms the term for cigarette butt into a symbol of dreary, mundane modern life. For Wellek and Warren, whether you saw "The Love Song" as ironical or not, this theme would become clear to any attentive reader. By the 1960s, however, the doctrine of immanence or "norms" was being questioned; the themes that emerged were seen to be, in part, a result of an implicit ideology shared by critics. Once the ideologies of formalism were exposed, the theory of norms was discarded, and new themes and different interpretations became more acceptable. Theory served to explain and defend various new approaches. The post-formalist was thus able to assert that Eliot's "butt-ends" need not evoke only a single theme; it could, for example, refer to the quotidian pleasures of daily life rather than to the spiritless quality of modern life. This book begins with deconstruction because in my view literary theory came into its own by way of the deconstruction of formalism.

The choice of theories for this book is personal, and a strong case could no doubt be made for an entirely different selection. With so many kinds of theory to choose from, consensus is unlikely. My selection is based on the belief that these six theories are fundamental for the theories that come after them and have already had a profound effect upon our culture.

The theories to be included are as follows. The book begins with an analysis of Jacques Derrida's conception of deconstruction because, although not a full-fledged theory, it provides a strategy used by all of the other theorists. Chapter Two looks at Michel Foucault's views on the disciplines of learning because the nature of knowledge is fundamental to any theory. The next issue, the communication of knowledge, is considered in Chapter Three on Wolfgang Iser's notion of reader response. Since knowledge in the humanities focuses upon people and the human dilemma, Chapter Four considers Jacques Lacan's concept of personal identity. Society and how we group and treat individuals are the subject of Chapter Five, a discussion of Fredric Jameson's new version of Marxism. Because the first five theorists are men, the last chapter focuses on Hélène Cixous's feminist view, an alternative to male theory. All the theorists included in this volume are from the period when literary theory was first recognized as a discipline. Their pioneering work forms the foundation, in my view, for what comes after them. I hope, in a companion volume, to analyze some of the more recent theorists who build upon and modify in innovative ways the work of their predecessors.

The order of the chapters also follows that suggested by deconstruction. If the norms or absolutes of criticism are called into question, the first and most basic issue is how do we reevaluate truth(s) communicated by art (Chapter Two). If no single ideology is privileged above others, how do different belief systems influence interpretation (Chapter Three)? Moreover, how do these different approaches change our concept of the ego and personal identity (Chapter Four)? The acceptance of diverse ideologies alters our political premises (Chapter Five). And finally, how is the female point of view to be understood and given a place in this new framework (Chapter Six)?

All the theories in this book are selected because they have a bearing upon both literary criticism and our daily lives. Deconstruction is seen as a strategy not a theory because it only serves an ethical end when used by some film-makers and theorists to go beyond Derrida. Foucault demonstrates that the pursuit of truth is not free but constricted by the cultural constructs or disciplines of knowledge. Lacan believes that the ego, our personal identity, is a function not of drives and instincts but of discourse, most notably language. Jameson asserts that the traditional Marxist dialectic of historical forces is altered by attention to the formal and structural properties of cultural artifacts, particularly literature. Cixous argues that theory itself is an unfolding process, undermining its own structure and cohesion.

Clearly, the issues of this book have an applicability beyond literature to life. Questions such as the nature of knowledge or truth, the function of personal response in interpretation, the structure of our being or ego, the nature of the forces of politics, the female alternative to the male view of the world, are fundamental for all of us, forming the basis of our civilization. As we see new cultures emerging out of oppression and totalitarianism, analysis of the relationship between literary theory and popular culture will help us understand our civilization and adapt it to the fast-changing world.

Theory arose in defense of difference, new ideas about truth and knowledge, new views of interpretation, a new concept of the ego, a new notion of political order, a new presentation of the feminine. Difference or otherness is the main problem in the world today, whether it be in the Mid-East fighting against tyranny or in our own cultures where minorities struggle for acceptance. Is it any wonder, then, that literary theory relates to popular culture?

Since this book arose in a pedagogical context, it seemed appropriate to include Suggestions for Teaching Literary Theory. Each chapter of the book is linked to a section devoted to a discussion on teaching these notions. But what seemed to work for me may not for others. We all have or develop our own style and voice in the classroom. Nevertheless, the use of films involved a reciprocal process. The students taught me how they see the world—a distinctly visual world—and I tried to learn how to place literary theory in that context. When successful, two worlds came into conversation, my textually oriented one and their visual one. The result, this book, crosses arts, genres, and generations. Theory is, I believe, the bridge that enables the conversation.

CHAPTER ONE

Deconstruction

Summary: I begin with deconstruction because all of the other theorists in the volume use it as a strategy. The first topic of discussion is decentering, illustrated by Christoph Waltz who plays SS officer Hans Lander in Quentin Tarantino's "Inglourious Basterds" (2009). The second key idea of Derrida's, originary myths, is described in relation to "Inglourious Basterds." Since Derrida's main contribution is his concept of metaphor, the second section uses "Kill Bill" to explain his view that death is inherent in metaphor. However, the third section, an analysis of "The Dark Knight," makes clear that the films move beyond deconstruction toward ethical ends. Another area where films move beyond deconstruction is history, considered in a discussion of "Inglourious Basterds." Two other uses of deconstruction for ethical ends are seen in "The Bourne Supremacy," the goal of which is personal integrity, and "Everyone Says I Love You," designed to highlight a new kind of friendship. The last two films, "Deconstructing Harry" and "Man of the Year," are examples of satirical uses of deconstruction, demonstrating in particular how deconstructing ones self may serve an ethical purpose.

This book begins with deconstruction for two reasons: 1) all of the theorists in the succeeding chapters use deconstruction as a strategy; 2) deconstruction in the context of film provides a means of relating literary theory to life, to the issues and problems of our everyday existence. In an interview, Derrida was asked what he thought of the term deconstruction being bandied about in common parlance. He replied that, even if people did not understand it as he would wish, the term must have some meaning in common usage and about that he was not unhappy. This chapter will show how the use of deconstruction by theorists is related to its applicability to daily life.

"Inglourious Basterds" (2009), starring Brad Pitt and Christoph Waltz, provides a vivid illustration of deconstruction. In fact, the central plot of this film demonstrates how a movie-maker and a cinema owner deconstruct Nazism. The story involves Hitler and his staff attending the premiere of a film about a German sniper who single-handedly killed nearly 300 Allied soldiers. Hence the film is entitled "Nation's Pride." During the viewing, the cinema is set on fire by a young woman whose family has been murdered by the Nazis. The fuel used is highly flammable old films. While burning alive, Hitler and his senior officers are shown a film made by the cinema owner informing her victims that they are dying at the hands of a Jew, who laughs as the cinema burns. The Nazi movie is one of Hitler's pet projects: he wishes to defeat David Selznick, the Jewish Hollywood mogul, at his own game. Tarantino turns the tables on Hitler. We see the Führer and his generals so enamored with the heroic exploits of the German sniper—as presumably we are by Tarantino's film—that they are unaware of the plot to kill them unfolding around them in the cinema.

Decentering and Christoph Waltz

The process being portrayed by Tarantino is basic to deconstruction, what Derrida calls "decentering." For Hitler and his staff, "Nation's Pride," the Nazi propaganda movie, is the heart of a project to convince the German army that they can win the war. For the Allies the film screening provides a means of destroying the Third Reich which, in a moment of self-congratulation (with the exception of one officer, who decides not to give the game away), is caught off guard. Derrida explains as follows: "At the center the permutation or transformation of elements [...] is forbidden. [...] Thus it has always been thought that the center, which is by definition unique, constituted that very thing within a structure which while governing a structure, escapes structurality [...]. The center is not the center" (*Structure*, 84). The German high command is unable to comprehend how "Nation's Pride" can be the center of a plan to destroy the command structure of the German army. The movie-house is another example of decentering in that it was conceived by the Germans as a refuge and made secure as such, but the Allies convert the secure refuge into a tomb, a fire trap that prevents escape. Tarantino's use of stylized violence, a hallmark of most of his films, is very much in evidence here. Prevented by the Nazis from doing his job because of his skin color, the "Negro" projectionist flips a cigarette into the pile of film reels, igniting the fire, while the "inglorious basterds" in the balcony machine-gun down the German officers. The carnage points up the surreal, fantasy-like quality of the scene: the point being not that this could have happened but that the imagined possibility is based upon changing the center from Hitler and his retinue to the cinema owner, the projectionist, and the "basterds." Turning Nazi power upon itself is not so much a historical possibility as an imaginative leap involving a violent questioning of customary assumptions—in this instance, that the Nazis can control the historical record. For the goal of deconstruction is not so much to subvert the establishment or change the state of things as to put accepted premises into play, to shake up our way of thinking.

The one German officer capable of such thinking, who understands how the enemy plans to use the cinema, is the Nazi SS officer, Hans Lander, the only German to anticipate and uncover the Allied plot. His ability at decentering is seen in the opening scene of the film. Known as the "Jew Hunter," he comes to a French farmhouse in search of a Jewish family. While Lander, brilliantly portrayed by Christoph Waltz, is interviewing the Frenchman in the farmhouse, the audience is shown the Dreyfus family hiding beneath the floorboards. Lander's speech and action illustrate deconstruction. First he explains his pride in his moniker, the "Jew Hunter," an achievement, he explains, that derives from thinking not like a German, but like a Jew. Germans, he continues, act like hawks and therefore expect Jews to hide in places a hawk might choose. Jews, on the other hand, behave like rats and therefore seek refuge in places where hawks would not expect them to be. He goes on to point out that it is no more offensive to characterize Jews as rats than to call him the "Jew Hunter." Both are merely adapting to their situation: Lander is doing his job and Jews are struggling to survive.

Having established that he is a hawk able to adopt the perspective of a rat, Lander makes clear that he knows the Frenchman is harboring a Jewish family on his property, but that if he cooperates his own family will be spared. Note that here Lander decenters the French farmer's focus, moving his concern from the Dreyfus family to his own family. Also, as we shall see, language is crucial in this scene. Lander, an adept linguist, begins the conversation with the Frenchman in French, then changes to English, understood by the Frenchman but not by the Jewish family. Having made his pact with the Frenchman in English, Lander reverts to French, stating, for the Jewish family to hear, that the investigation is over. Upon leaving, he orders his men in German to machine-gun the unsuspecting family beneath the floor. As we shall see, language and the manipulation of words is a key element of deconstruction.

Here we note that decentering is a basic principle of deconstruction. Any position, whether physical or intellectual, contains within itself the means of its own undoing: Derrida often uses the term "seams" to suggest the vulnerability of any human construct. In this scene from "Inglorious Basterds" the process is compounded, for the Jews have replaced the center of the German hawk with that of the rat, and Lander, anticipating this form of deconstruction, has discovered the hiding place of the Jews. This episode makes clear that the decentered is not immune to deconstruction, to being itself decentered. This point is key to the main plot of "Inglourious Basterds" where, as we have already suggested, Hitler's attempt to decenter David Selznick is itself decentered by Tarantino. For this reason deconstruction is, in my view, not a theory but a strategy that serves theory: any position arrived at by way of deconstruction is itself susceptible to being deconstructed, so any ethical move goes beyond the realm of deconstruction. I shall demonstrate that the movies used in this chapter to illustrate deconstruction in the end go beyond it, and that the theorists in subsequent chapters who use deconstruction also conclude by moving to a different level.

Originary myths and "Inglourious Basterds"

For our purposes, two important ideas emerge from deconstruction. One is decentering, illustrated in the above example, and the other is that of the originary myth. The two are related in that the center implies a story or an account explaining its centrality and a narrative involving a beginning or an origin. Derrida coins the term deconstruction to suggest a process neither destructive nor reconstructive, but a technique that oscillates or, to use Derrida's term, "plays" between the two for the purpose of questioning or "decentering" accepted dichotomies and exposing the mythic elements of explanations of origins. The goal of this analysis involves uncovering what Derrida calls forms of mastery. For instance, Lander points out to the farmer that our abhorrence of rats versus hawks is irrational, without empirical evidence, and thus we are prepared for Lander to alter his attitude at the end, recognizing the hawk-like quality of some Jews.

Addressing this issue in one of his early well-known works, "Structure, Sign and Play in the Discourse of the Human Sciences," Derrida deconstructs the analysis of the famous anthropologist, Claude Lévi-Strauss, whose view of cultural myths is based upon the distinction between "raw and cooked," a variation on the nature/nurture dichotomy, that is, inherited or instinctive qualities versus learned behavior. Derrida demonstrates that Lévi-Strauss's account of the distinction between raw and cooked actually shows that the two are never completely divorced from one another. Hence, Derrida makes much of Lévi-Strauss's remark that there is no society without the incest taboo, a statement that leads to questions about the distinction between raw and cooked, since it cannot be determined whether the incest taboo is a result of nature or nurture. As a constant, the incest taboo may be solely a function of nurture, each culture following the one before it, or the result of nature, an element inherent in the human gene pool. Derrida's point is that Lévi-Strauss's raw–cooked dualism is not an empirical phenomenon, a natural occurrence, but a pattern devised for the purpose of interpreting nature.

What Derrida means by pattern or model is provided by Tarantino's presentation of his signature as interpreter in the form of chapter titles and volume numbers, a device used in both of his movies discussed in this chapter, to interrupt vivid, violent images with printed language. Like a bespectacled librarian wandering misguidedly onto a movie set, these insertions of printed words on the screen serve to remind the audience that, despite the appearance of mayhem and chaos, these films are written with an artistic purpose. We are thus encouraged to interpret, to read, in every sense of the term, the visual events before us. Although we may be tempted to believe that a film with fast-paced action and clipped dialogue is largely improvised, the written word leads us to question that assumption. And the juxtaposition of oral and written language is reminiscent of Derrida's analysis of this dichotomy.

Another influential work by Derrida, dating from the 1970s, about assumptions, *Of Grammatology*, considers the concept of "originary myths," that is, unexamined beliefs about or accounts of beginnings which are taken as factual or beyond dispute but which, according to Derrida, involve interpretation. His prime example is the belief that speech precedes writing. We take for granted from the Biblical account of the creation of the universe that God said, rather than wrote, "let there be light." But Derrida points out that the documents cited to demonstrate the original orality of early cultures, whether the ancient epics or scriptural texts, such as the Bible or the Koran, are written works and make reference to writing, so that we lack conclusive evidence that speech predated writing. Derrida's point is not that writing preceded speech. That would itself be another absolute dichotomy, or what Derrida would call a "binarism" subject to deconstruction. Rather, he wishes to put into play the speech–writing dichotomy and question the mutual exclusivity of either. Why? Because Derrida asserts that all human constructs favor one origin over another for purposes of power. Philosophical ideas are never neutral but involve what Derrida calls the "privileging" of some elements over others. All human constructs involve hierarchies of power that for the most part favor the establishment. However, putting the absolutes—the accepted binarisms and originary myths—into play does not necessarily for Derrida involve reversal or revolution, because the alternative is equally subject to deconstruction.

In *Of Grammatology* Derrida re-examines the assumption of Ferdinand de Saussure, a key thinker for structuralism, the French version of formalism, that oral language determines the structure of written language:

One should, moreover, say *model* rather than *structure*; it is not a question of a system constructed and functioning perfectly, but of an ideal explicitly directing a functioning which *in fact* is never completely phonetic. [...] it does not respond to any necessity of an absolute and universal essence (*Of Grammatology*, 39).

Because an interpretive decision, not an objective description, is involved, Derrida prefers the term "model" to "structure." Other models could have been selected. For Derrida, phonetics, the basis of Saussure's model, cannot bolster any claim for linguistics as a science. Rather, linguistics based upon phonetics is an influential theory founded upon an interpretation privileging the oral over the written. The term "grammatology" is offered as an alternative to Saussure's "semiology," his version of linguistics as a science of linguistics that privileges the oral over the written. Grammatology applies to both speech and writing, leaving open the question of origin.

The advantage of this substitution will not only be to give to the theory of writing the scope needed to counter logocentric repression and the subordination to linguistics. It will liberate the semiological project itself from what, in spite of its greater theoretical extension, remained *governed* by linguistics, organized as if linguistics were at once its center and its telos. *Even though semiology was in fact more general and comprehensive than linguistics, it continued to be regulated as if it were one of the areas of linguistics. The linguistic sign remained exemplary of semiology*, it dominated it as the master-sign and as the generative model: the pattern (*Of Grammatology*, 51).

Again, Derrida is not reversing the hierarchy to herald a linguistics of the written as the new science. Instead, he asserts that decisions about which one takes precedence must not be taken for granted but be based upon sound argument or interpretation. The title "Inglourious Basterds" is illustrative both of the playfulness of language and of the sort of binarisms that interest Derrida. The "inglourious basterds" are the polar opposite of Hans Lander. Adept at four languages, Lander is a well educated, sophisticated, and urbane European; the "basterds" are fearless and forthright American Jews but for their leader First Lieutenant Aldo Raine, a tough country boy who takes no prisoners. The mission of the basterds is to beat to death with a baseball bat and scalp Nazis. Tarantino continually plays with this contrast between European finesse and American bluntness. One of the more memorable moments of the film is when Aldo Raine and two of his cohorts pretend to be Italian and Lander exposes the deception by speaking volubly to them in fluent Italian. Tarantino, however, goes beyond Derrida in not being content to toy with and upset the balance of this European–American dichotomy. The title, "Inglourious Basterds," indicates that

Tarantino sides with the uncouth Americans, who not only beat the Nazis but also brand them with a swastika, an ethical move to be considered later in this chapter. And the misspelling in the title—errors that would be more likely to be associated with the less well-educated Americans—reinforces the point that Tarantino sides with Aldo Raine and his gang. In fact, Terantino stated on the Dave Letterman show that the misspelling of the title was "his spelling," and Tarantino has made clear that he regards this film as his masterpiece, the very words Aldo Raine uses at the end of the movie when a swastika is carved on the forehead of Hans Lander.

For purposes of literary analysis, deconstruction is most useful in the context of the analysis of metaphor, and the most important piece that Derrida has written in this regard is one first published in English in *New Literary History*, entitled "White Mythology: Metaphor in the Text of Philosophy." What Derrida means by metaphor is clear from the literary example he offers early in his essay. In Anatole France's *The Garden of Epicurus*, one of the characters offers a metaphor for the language of metaphysicians:

Instead of knives and scissors [metaphysicians] [...] should put medals and coins to the grindstone to efface [them] until nothing is visible in their crown-pieces, [...] neither King Edward, nor the Emperor William, nor the Republic [...] having nothing either English, German, nor French. [...] By this knife-grinder's activity words are changed from a physical to a metaphysical acceptation ("White Mythology," 7–8).

Since metaphor is a key factor in literature, some think the most important one of all, Derrida shows how deconstruction applies to literary criticism. The overall importance of metaphor in all discourse is made quite clear throughout the essay: "it is not so much that metaphor is in the text [...] rather these texts are in metaphor" ("White Mythology," 60). The point here is not that literature is one huge metaphor, but that the necessarily interpretive nature of metaphor is characteristic of all literature. The implication is that metaphor cannot be escaped or transcended; no single generalization or overriding conception can be found that permits mastery by philosophy or any other discipline. In Derrida's terms there can be no metaphor of metaphors. Why not? Because the moment one establishes a metaphor of metaphors, it is subject to deconstruction.

The purpose of this assertion is to emphasize the function of interpretation, to highlight the basis for decisions about origins and the privileging of one side of a dichotomy, since a literary trope is usually seen as not straightforward but calling for a reading or interpretation. For example, one of the most famous metaphors is Dante's multifoliate rose, traditionally seen as an image of love. The thorns of the rose are usually viewed as the trials and tribulations of courtship and romance. But Derrida suggests that metaphor "always has its own death within it" ("White Mythology," 74), providing for the possibility that the multifoliate rose could be seen as a symbol of anti-love or indifference, as disinterested as the thorn is in the wounded thumb. Again, the point is not to reverse the traditional assumption about love but to point out that it is just that, an assumption based upon an unexamined interpretation. And lest we are tempted to think of the multifoliate rose as the metaphor of metaphors, one need only imagine a skillful poet using the rambler rose, the single-layered flower, to represent everything Dante presented with the multifoliate one. This notion that metaphor can never be encapsulated or contained within some larger concept is at the very heart of literature, literary criticism, and literary theory. Any attempt at a metaphor of metaphors becomes another metaphor subject to deconstruction, that is, it can be appropriated by an artist to subvert the philosophic attempt at mastery or totality. Imagine someone attending to this analysis drawing a picture of single and multifoliate roses so entwined as to prevent either from thriving—a metaphor of this description of metaphor.

Death and "Kill Bill"

The death inherent in metaphor, the thorns of the rose, is a central consideration for Derrida, including but going well beyond literary criticism:

> This death no doubt, is also the death of philosophy. But this "of" may be taken in two ways. Sometimes the death of philosophy is the death of a particular philosophical form in which philosophy itself is reflected on and summed up and in which philosophy, reaching its fulfillment, comes face to face with itself. But sometimes the death of philosophy is the death of a philosophy which does not see itself die, and never more finds itself ("White Mythology," 74).

Death here means change in the historical sense of variation and evolution from the past, a human world of unfolding ideas, a civilization or civilizations questioning its own basic assumptions.

Perhaps because deconstruction focuses upon a concept of metaphor with death at its core, Quentin Tarantino's movies are particularly apt illustrations. I shall first examine "Kill Bill" Volumes I and II (2003–4), and then return to "Inglourious Basterds" (2009). "Kill Bill," starring Uma Thurman and David Carradine, focuses upon the relationship between death and birth, in particular between assassination and pregnancy: the opening scene, the key to the plot of the film, presents Bea telling Bill that she is pregnant with his child as he shoots her. In fact, all the main characters are trained killers who have few moral scruples about their victims except when these are children. Even when Bill, the leader of the group, kills or believes he has killed Bea he saves and nurtures her daughter. If "Kill Bill" is a metaphor of assassination, killing is decentered by Bea's child *in utero*. In the first episode after the opening scene, Chapter Two, Bea discovers that she is pregnant with Bill's child. She has been sent on an assignment by Bill to kill a woman who in turn sends an assassin to kill Bea. When the two female killers meet in a hotel room with guns drawn, Bea asks her counterpart to look at the pregnancy test. Convinced of the truth of Bea's claim, the other assassin agrees to leave without firing her gun. But this soft center of motherly love does not hold; it is in free play with death, particularly near the end when Bea murders Bill not so much because of his attempt on her life as for not informing her of the survival of her daughter. The final line of Volume One is Bill's question: does Bea know about her daughter? Tarantino thus suggests that mothering and murdering are somehow related in a strange way, capable of deconstructing one another. On the one hand, Bea decides to assassinate Bill for, or so she assumes until the final chapter, murdering her unborn child. On the other hand, in the very next episode, Chapter Three, Bea in the presence of a four-year-old girl kills the child's mother, who was part of the group that attacked the wedding party. However, although it may appear that mothering and murdering are in free play in a dynamic equilibrium where one or the other predominates at different moments, Tarantino, as we shall see, in the end weighs the balance in favor of mothering: Bill dies because he violated the maternal instinct.

The most startling discovery for me was that this violent film about assassins achieves resolution·with mother and child. But then my attitude toward the violence changed after viewing "Kill Bill" a second time. My students had explained that the violence of Tarantino is stylized, but at my first viewing I felt assaulted. After watching the film for the second and third time, I found myself laughing at scenes that at first horrified me. Gamesomeness and play are hallmarks of deconstruction. The very fact that "Kill Bill" portrays killers who regard childhood as sacrosanct renders the entire film a sort of fantasy game, most obviously in the swordfights, particularly when Bea single-handedly defeats the entire "Gang of 88." But even when Bea kills a mother in the presence of the victim's daughter, she not only spares the child, a witness to her capital crime, but tells the youngster that when she grows up she will have the right to avenge her mother's death. The result is a scene of premeditated murder and bizarre comedy. A professional assassin mothers the child of her victim. Bea's nurturing instinct combined with her Amazonian swordsmanship serve to make her the heroine of the film; as the narrator she shows and tells us how she conquered Bill and his gang, a victory that is, as we shall see, literally a two-edged sword.

In order to beat Bill at his own game she needs a Honso sword and Pai Mei's lethal five-finger maneuver. And here we confront Derrida's concept of an originary myth. Why do Honso and Pai Mei help Bea kill Bill? Honso has made a sword for Bill that is shown early on in the film before we see Bill, suggesting that it is key to his personality, and Pai Mei has trained Bill, told him about the technique, but taught it not to him but to Bea. We are not given answers to these questions but can only assume that these masters of the sword and unarmed lethal combat believe that what Bill did to Bea was wrong. Tarantino's myth of origin is an ethical principle: he devotes his skill as a film-maker and writer to a comic fantasy about how an assassin/mother can use her abilities as a trained killer and her rage as a child protector to get revenge against Bill and his gang. But the complication here is that Bea's enemy is family in a literal and surrogate sense. Not only is Bill the father of her child but also the rest of the gang are surrogate aunts and uncles. Indeed, Bill's brother is referred to by Bea as "Uncle Budd." Moreover, she has, we are told at the wedding rehearsal, no other family. Deconstruction is so clearly illustrated in this film because the other, the enemy, is intimately bound up with Bea herself.

The main characters comprise the family that Bill calls "Natural Born Killers." This phrase applies to Bill's gang of personally trained assassins and is a reference to Tarantino's screenplay of that name revised in 1994 by Oliver Stone into the famous and controversial film using the same title. The family nature of violence in "Kill Bill 2" is made clear at the outset when Bea "aka Mommy" explains that she seeks revenge against Bill, the master killer who trained her to kill and then attempted to kill her. But that of course is another originary myth, for we are left to wonder where this killer instinct came from, what is its source. The closest we come to an answer to this question is in the last chapter of the film when we meet B.B., the daughter of Bea and Bill. B.B. tells her mother that when she saw her goldfish flopping on the carpet she decided to step on it instead of putting it back in the water. What are we to make of this story? Are we to see the child as a natural-born killer or is this sort of childhood cruelty all too familiar to parents and schoolteachers? Or, since Bill encourages B.B. to tell the story, is it Bill's originary myth, his twisted attempt to justify not telling Bea about B.B. because she is another natural born killer? Any of these explanations of the origins of the assassins is hardly adequate, especially since it is doubtful that either Bill or Bea had a childhood like that of B.B. Derrida uses Emmanuel Levinas's formulation to describe this phenomenon: "a past that never was and can never will be, whose future to come will never be a *production* or a reproduction in the form of presence" (*Of Grammatology*, 71). Bea and Bill have no past beyond that shown in the film because Tarantino wants them to have no family except that of the gang. Why? To portray the absolute otherness of the family killer, a cold-blooded assassin within the family. Tarantino's interest in this paradox begins to become clear in Volume Two.

This second part opens with perhaps the most shocking scene of the film when "Uncle Budd" buries Bea alive. Why does he choose this cruel form of death? Budd was one of the group at the end of "Kill Bill, Volume I" that gunned down the marriage party, and, as Budd later says to Bill, Bea deserves her revenge. So he waits for Bea to come after him, shoots her in the breast with rock salt to "settle her down," then buries her alive, explaining that he is thus achieving revenge for his brother Bill, who felt betrayed when Bea chose to marry and leave the gang. Burying Bea alive is a vivid example of decentering. A seething mass of anger, Bea seeks revenge upon Budd for following the orders of Bill; Budd imprisons her in a casket, leaving her to stew in her own corrosive anger. Instead of merely killing her, Budd makes Bea her own assassin, expecting that she will exhaust her meager supply of air with hate and venom and so expire, in a sense, by way of her obsession with revenge. He even supplies her with a flashlight, presumably so that she can, so to speak, see her own death. But, as we would expect, any form of deconstruction is itself subject to deconstruction, so Bea's drive for revenge is channeled into the martial arts taught her by the master, Pai Mei, who trained her to use her hands to break through wood. Pai Mei is also the source of another form of deconstruction in that, as we mentioned earlier, Bill dies by way of a technique Bea learned from Pai Mei, who was introduced to Bea by Bill. Tarantino gives the episode of Bea's training by Pai Mei a separate chapter with the title "The Master," suggesting the decentering of Bill by Bill. Moreover, to continue with the surrogate family motif, in killing Bill, Bea's first master, Bea murders someone who is her master/trainer as well as her lover and the father of her child.

The stylized violence of "Kill Bill, Volume 2" functions to remind us that no one is better able to provoke anger and aggression than friends and family members who know how to produce rage and hatred or to evoke laughter and love. There are numerous examples in the movie of predictable reactions. Perhaps the most prominent is the death of Uncle Budd. Elle Driver, a family or gang member, brings Budd the money for the Honso sword in a suitcase full of cash. She knows that Budd is so enamored with the money that he will be unable to resist opening the case to count it and revel in his new wealth, allowing the black mamba inside to bite him repeatedly in the face. Surprisingly, this physically violent scene is literary in a savagely comical way; like a research assistant reporting her findings Elle Driver reads her notes about the black mamba to Budd, writhing in anguish. Action and thought, speech and writing contaminate one another in a context of free play. Moving the center from money to Budd, Elle decides, instead of assassinating him, to let him do himself in, much as Budd did with Bea. But she is herself subject to the same force she unleashes on Budd. Bea finally defeats Driver by plucking out her other eye—another technique that Bea learned from Pai Mei who had put out Driver's eye for the same kind of arrogant disrespect that Driver displayed toward Bea. Finally, now blind and left in the trailer home with the black mamba, Elle is likely to die by way of the very means of death she devised for Budd.

At the end of "Kill Bill 2" we see the gradual deconstruction of the family. Bea has killed Bill to protect her daughter from her father. But in the end power is not merely reversed. Bea does not take Bill's place as head of the natural born killers. She lies on the bathroom floor cuddling a teddy bear, laughing and crying at the same time, having lost a lover, husband and father to her child, and having overcome her most powerful enemy. But her future is uncertain. Will she be content to be a mother to her daughter who perhaps shows ominous signs of the killer instinct? Will Bea be able to lead a new gang of assassins and also raise a child? Power when deconstructed is not so much altered as thrown into question, shaken from its moorings. A woman has replaced a man, but she has the added responsibility of a child.

Nevertheless, the conclusion of "Kill Bill, Vol. 2" seems to me to suggest a move beyond deconstruction. At the end of the film, Bea has accepted her responsibility as a mother, and in this respect her motive for revenge is, unlike that of the other gang members, not merely personal. As the narrator and "heroine" of the film, Bea has an element of personal integrity respected by Honso and Pai Mei that cannot be attributed to anyone else in the film. Why motherhood is valued is not made clear in "Kill Bill." Tarantino clarifies his ethical position in his next film, "Inglourious Basterds." In fact, the ethical positions developed in the other films in this chapter will become a central concern: moving beyond Derrida, these films thus suggest the function of deconstruction in our lives.

Deconstruction toward an ethical end: "The Dark Knight"

By now it should be clear that the key idea in this chapter on decon-struction—my center—combines decentering and the exposure of myths of origin. Film-makers uncover the "seams" or vulnerabilities of any human construct that can then be used, going beyond Derrida, to alter the central or core idea, leading to a conclusion opposite to that of the original intent. This particular use of deconstruction enables some movie-makers to relate deconstruction to our daily lives. A good cinematic illustration in the context of political power is Christopher Nolan's "The Dark Knight" (2008), starring Christian Bale as Batman and Heath Ledger as the "Joker." In this sequel to "Batman Begins," the "Joker" is one of many fascinated with Batman. But unlike the others who try to imitate Batman, the "Joker" deconstructs him, a point made clear in the opening scene of the film. Leading a bank robbery, the "Joker" kills all of his accomplices, so that like Batman he is ridding Gotham City of the bad guys, but not for the good of the city. Rather he is demonstrating his own playful prowess—his shooting of his accomplices is not unlike that of a child wielding a toy gun—and precluding the possibility of being turned in by any member of the gang. Although Batman can easily unmask his other imitators by anticipating their actions, the "Joker" presents a greater challenge, for he neither wishes to displace Batman nor to reconstruct him in his own image. In fact, the "Joker" explains in a confrontation with Batman that he does not kill him because he needs him, for the "free play" of a binary relationship, which is, as we have seen, a key idea for deconstruction.

But "The Dark Knight" is particularly interesting because it concludes with a reversal of the power hierarchy. Batman grooms Harvey Dent, the DA, to take over the job of controlling crime in Gotham City. But when the "Joker" arranges for the capture of Dent's lover, Rachel Dawes, the assistant DA, Dent turns on Batman and the law enforcers because the "Joker" reveals that Rachel could have been saved if she had not been betrayed by a corrupt police force. In the end, Batman prevents Dent from killing the family of the police commissioner. However, Batman and the commissioner recognize that Batman will have to take responsibility for all of Dent's crimes so that the people of Gotham City will not lose hope. The "Joker" has thus deconstructed Batman's daytime persona, Bruce Wayne, who at the beginning was at the top of society, a successful and influential businessman. Wayne is now the outcast, the dark knight.

The "Joker" achieves this feat by insisting that Batman unmask himself, reveal his origin. Batman, however, refuses to show his true face even if the price exacted by the "Joker" is exile to darkness, loss of daytime status, becoming a denizen of the night. Why? Batman cannot allow himself to be seen for what he is, a member of the establishment, a wealthy businessman and playboy-bachelor. He would lose credibility in Gotham City, and all of his acts of altruism to save his society and its individuals could be seen as the ultimately self-serving preservation of the world in which Batman is one of the top men. Of course, this inversion of the power hierarchy is itself subject to deconstruction: we are assured that Batman will exploit his new marginalized position to do what he has always done, to use the black mask to protect the people of Gotham City. In this sense, the "Joker," the deconstructor, does not prevail, so Batman can carry on with his good work even if he must, because of the "Joker," maintain a lower profile.

But the film is entitled "The Dark Knight" and not "Batman II" because the "Joker" has radically altered Batman's style; he has to close down his daytime existence. Bruce Wayne is out of business. I wonder if this change represents the deep skepticism of present-day society, the belief that any form of decency, any act of altruism, may be subject to deconstruction, may become the opposite of what it seems. Perhaps that is why the "Joker" also maintains his mask, as if deconstruction threatens to show us that good and evil are all too ordinary, living in and amongst us, knowledge Batman fears will lead to general despair. Yet Batman's new existence on the margins suggests that he will now become a deconstructor by profession. Nonetheless, "The Dark Knight" concludes with an ethical position beyond deconstruction: the price of helping to save society may entail being alienated from it because most people have lost all faith in the altruism of any member of the establishment.

The historical goals of the "Inglourious Basterds"

One of the questions often raised about deconstruction is that, while undermining traditional goals, it does not seem to forward any of its own; in philosophical terms it questions any telos but has itself no telos. While that is generally true, and indeed it is for that reason that I referred earlier to deconstruction as a strategy rather than a theory, the most recent Tarantino movie does suggest more overtly than "Kill Bill, Vol. 2" how deconstruction can be employed toward a new goal.

The opening scene of "Inglourious Basterds," as we have seen, exemplifies deconstruction. But I now wish to isolate the ethical element of this film, how Tarantino's conclusion moves beyond deconstruction and relates to our lives. Specifically, Hans Lander represents a new telos. Christoph Waltz, the Austrian actor playing Lander, received the Best Actor Award at the Cannes film festival and an Academy Award for his role in this film. The great acting feat here lies in showing us how a Nazi can survive the war and the defeat of Germany by deconstructing himself. Lander not only deconstructs himself but also shows viewers of the film that he is deconstructing himself.

Let us return again to the opening scene. Lander explains that he earned his nickname by doing what other Nazis are incapable of, namely putting himself in the position of the Jew. During this explanation he is filling his pen like an obsessively methodical Nazi, thus epitomizing to the audience the stereotype that he is deconstructing. He maintains the role of Nazi bureaucrat for the Frenchman and the Germans under his command while at the same time adopting the opposite role to capture the Jews, thereby maintaining his reputation as the "Jew Hunter."

One further element of this scene now requires comment. All the members of the Jewish family are killed except for the adolescent daughter Shoshanna, who escapes. It is not clear in the movie why Lander allows her to escape, since we see that he has her clearly in the sights of his gun.

Perhaps Shoshanna on the run is a challenge for Lander, indicated by his remark at the end of the scene, "Au revoir, Shoshanna." In any event, thoroughness, a common Nazi trait, is here (playfully) put into play, for Lander lets her go but never gives up the pursuit of her: in Derridean terms, being thoroughly unthorough.

We next see them together four years later in Paris where Shoshanna, now a grown woman with a different name, is managing a movie theatre that is to be used by high-ranking Nazi officials, including Hitler himself. Lander is in charge of security. The conversation between the two protagonists is in my view a brilliant acting performance on both their parts because each is playing with dual identities—Lander, chief of security and murderer of the Dreyfus family, and Shoshanna, the young Jewish girl he may recognize and the French owner of the cinema charmed by the German officer. The deconstructive tour de force here is that the audience sees the free play between the identities of each character. First Lander adopts the part of the charming officer speaking immaculate, polite French to the owner of the cinema. He then orders a glass of milk, as he had done at the farmhouse in the past, indicating to Shoshanna that he recognizes her and has her in his power. Shoshanna first responds with upright dignity to the polite correctness of the officer and then, when the milk is ordered, adopts a more circumspect attitude. Each is responding to and attempting to manipulate the other, neither knowing for certain what the other is planning to do. We never know why Lander does not arrest Shoshanna. Is he still fascinated with the challenge of following her progress or does he now begin to feel that the tide is turning in her favor? One is tempted to wonder whether the "Jew Hunter" suspects that she and her kind may one day reverse the hierarchy on the Nazis.

Later on in the movie Lander discovers that British and American soldiers, with the help of some of the local resistance members, have set up a trap that will kill all the people inside the cinema. Instead of foiling the plot, he decides to use his knowledge of it as a bargaining chip to avoid being tried as a war criminal after the end of hostilities. And the movie concludes with Lander making his deal allowing the allies to blow up the theater. But, although he survives, Lander is shocked and scandalized when Aldo Raine, the head of the American squad of Nazi scalpers, carves a swastika in his forehead, leaving a lifelong reminder of his Nazi past. Lander, the deconstructor, is marked for life as an SS Colonel.

What is one to conclude from this playfulness concerning the sacred subject of the Holocaust, particularly as Hitler and his top brass are destroyed in a fire ignited by old movie reels—a directorial act of deconstruction? Tarantino is reported to have characterized the film as a "spaghetti western with a WWII iconography," but the WWII war movie genre is not merely parodied. Lander escapes and he does not; he survives but with a swastika branded on his forehead. And we are left to wonder if those Nazis who actually survived after the war, most notably in South America—like the infamous Mengele—slipped through the net because they too were clever and adroit like Lander, able to anticipate what we would expect Nazis to do, and thus escape by using Lander's strategy of deconstructing themselves.

For when the authorities eventually catch up with Nazis who have evaded prosecution, we usually find they are not fundamentally changed people. Think of Adolph Eichmann. In this respect, Christoph Waltz more than earns his best actor awards because, while adopting many different roles, speaking immaculate German, English, French, and Italian in pursuit of his duties as an SS Colonel and then changing to become an accomplice in the plot to kill Hitler, he remains the same character. For Waltz, the achievement is the actor acting the actor, and for Lander the adroit use of deconstruction applied to himself. Moreover, the deliberate misspelling of the movie's title is reminiscent of Derrida's coinage of key terms like deconstruction and "Differance." Derrida invents terms that cross binary borders, as deconstruction oscillates between destruction and reconstruction, and "Differance" plays between difference and deferral. Tarantino's title suggests that, while the main characters do behave like "Inglourious Basterds," they are anything but that. Although illiterate and lacking the finesse of Lander, the "Jew Hunter," the basterds nevertheless prevail. As we have seen, Tarantino's title plays on a familiar binarism: European sophisticated diplomacy (Christoph Waltz) versus American brash power (Brad Pitt). Tarantino concludes that Lander's scar prevents his escape to a quiet life on Nantucket Island. He must live with his past, something he can never deconstruct. At the end of the film Aldo Raine (Brad Pitt) permanently marks Lander's place in history, a fate Mengele and many other Nazis evaded. Here Tarantino uses deconstruction to go beyond it to make an ethical point, a position that is certainly not prominent in the early and most influential writings of Derrida, but is pursued by filmmakers using deconstructive strategies. History, Tarantino suggests, cannot be evaded by deconstruction; the destruction of the Nazis in the film is fanciful, but the indelible mark of the history of the Holocaust haunts our imagination.

Personal integrity in "The Bourne Supremacy"

Ethics takes the form of personal integrity in the thriller, directed by Paul Greengrass and starring Matt Damon, entitled "The Bourne Supremacy" (2004). Here we see that decentering involves not only changing the center, altering who or what is the focal point, but also moving what was in the center to the margins. Having been framed, Bourne can only survive the government attempts "to take him out" by evading the CIA, retreating from prominence to obscurity. Accordingly, the key moments in the film are when Bourne is looking at the CIA looking at him. In two instances, Bourne is on the roof across from the Berlin CIA headquarters looking at Pamela Landy and her crew watching their myriad computer monitors searching for Bourne, unaware that he is near enough to observe them through a rifle sight. Bourne's plan—and this is the key to his "supremacy" and the main plot line of the film—is to change the center of the CIA probe from Bourne to the CIA itself. By this means, Bourne hopes to shine light on corruption in the agency and to marginalize himself so that he can slip away into a quiet private life.

Bourne can manage this adroit decentering maneuver because, as a trained CIA agent, he anticipates what they will do and how they will proceed. In looking down the rifle sight at the CIA, he is, in effect, using their "bead" on him to see them. Why do the CIA people never realize that Jason Bourne is capable of deconstructing their plans first to "take him out" and then to "bring him in"? The CIA is always one step behind him because its people assume that Bourne is what they have trained him to be, an assassin, one devoted only to killing. And indeed Bourne is a successful assassin. But to survive as an assassin one must also be equally adept at evading other assassins who are likely to be sent in reprisal. A successful assassin must be a deconstructor of assassins.

Bourne can only survive physically by anticipating how the CIA plans to assassinate him and can only cope psychologically by deprogramming himself as an assassin. So he watches the CIA through a telescopic sight of a rifle that he never fires. Finally, at the end of the movie Bourne maneuvers Pamela Landy into the realization that the real culprit is her coworker, Ward Abbott, who has misled her about Bourne. He successfully decenters Landy's investigation. Eventually she accepts that Bourne may be something more than a mere killer. But even Pamela, straight and uncorrupt, attempts to bring Bourne in, on the assumption that a CIA agent needs the agency as a home. Bourne, however, surprises Pamela with words indicating that he has deconstructed himself as an assassin. Again looking at her from the rifle sight, he replies: "You look tired, Pam, get some rest."

The movie ends with Jason Bourne walking away, having freed himself from the dichotomy between the CIA and its agent, master and slave, an escape only possible because the establishment assumed that the agent would always remain the tool of the master establishment. What does Bourne accomplish by walking away? Not much. He cannot bring back the Neskis whom he killed under orders from the CIA, but he can at least tell their daughter the truth about how they died and accept responsibility for it. Deconstruction does not serve to destroy or redesign the system—in this instance, the CIA; nor does it reconstruct an alternative. It can open up a bit of free play, room for individual maneuver. In telling the Neskis' daughter what happened and that he pulled the trigger, Bourne can hope to recapture some self-respect; instead of covering up, like the CIA, he admits to his crime and faces the only survivor. Now perhaps he has enough personal integrity to sleep more soundly. Again, the movie suggests how deconstruction can lead to an ethical position that has some practical consequences for Bourne in his attempt to become a normal member of society. But of course the CIA can deconstruct Bourne by asserting that he is merely using the agency as an excuse for his illegal behavior. Bourne's move into private life does not escape the free play of deconstruction, but he can make the ethical decision to stop participating in it.

Comic deconstruction: "Everyone Says I Love You"

In a comic genre, Woody Allen's "Everyone Says I Love You," released in 1996 and starring Goldie Hawn, Julia Roberts, and Alan Alda, demonstrates how deconstruction applies in a context of love and friendship. At first this film seems to be a parody, in that all of the songs including the title song are old favorites from previous films and are sung by actors and actresses who are not trained singers or known for their voices. In fact, Allen was so intent on getting "ordinary voices" that he told Goldie Hawn that her voice was too good and Drew Barrymore that hers was worse than "ordinary." The ordinary voice serves to bring the romantic songs down to earth or into the mundane world, which is emphasized by altering the context of the songs. Two of the most obvious examples are "Makin' Whoopee" set in a maternity ward, and "Just You Just Me" at Harry Winston's Jewelers on Fifth Avenue. Also suggestive of parody is the fact that the love plot is completely phony. Woody Allen as Joe is given private information from Von's psychiatrist so that he can pretend to share her artistic knowledge and interests.

But the plot and the songs are handled too delicately for parody. The staging and presentation of the songs makes clear that Allen loves them, and the resolution reinforces that point. Von (Julia Roberts) ultimately leaves Joe (Woody Allen) because when her dream man comes true she no longer has a dream. So the romance of romantic musical comedy is reinforced. The conclusion of the film takes place in Paris on the banks of the Seine near the Pont Neuf. Steffie (Goldie Hawn) sings "I'm thru with Love" and she and Joe reminisce about their divorce and subsequent friendship. Steffie's dance involves impossible leaps with the wires holding her up vaguely visible. Yet the kiss between them is tender and touching; a failed marriage has produced a deep friendship. The deconstructive technique—oscillation between two extremes of parody and sentimentality neither of which is ever fully realized—serves to highlight a new kind of relationship. The point is not that Joe and Steffie will never be a couple again; rather, they maintain a friendship while pursuing love and marriage elsewhere. The result is a new kind of relationship, friendship between "exes," divorcees who grow closer to one another after divorce. Once again, film illustrates the use of deconstruction but moves beyond it: divorcees, Allen suggests, often know one another better than acquaintances, even than most friends, and can therefore form enduring bonds different from but just as deeply felt as marital love. This expanded notion of friendship—the companionableness of those once married—is best exemplified by having ordinary actors sing the songs, similar to the kind of singing that happens at parties of friends, usually slightly off-key around a piano ringing out the occasional wrong note. In reality, Allen implies, the music of friends oscillates between the ridiculous and the sublime, resting with neither. And that is where we live and form our closest human bonds. Once again deconstruction is used for a purpose beyond deconstruction. This new kind of friendship—important in present-day societies where the divorce rate is about 50 percent—is presented as a stable value not subject to free play.

Satirical deconstruction: "Deconstructing Harry" and "Man of the Year"

The last two films to be considered are comedies that illustrate the close relationship between satirical humor and deconstruction. Specifically, the first movie examines the intermingling of life and writing of a comic writer and the second shows the role of satire in politics. In 1997, Woody Allen produced a film entitled "Deconstructing Harry," starring Woody Allen and Robin Williams. The problem for Harry is that, in using elements from his own life in his writing, he risks alienating friends and family. For instance, in the opening scene, Harry's ex-girlfriend threatens to shoot him because a character in one of his stories is, in her view, a veiled version of herself that shows her in an unflattering light. Ironically, Harry is a successful writer but leads a miserable life. We see from various vignettes of his writing that he focuses upon himself as the butt of his humor; he becomes so accustomed to self-satire that he is surprised when his friends and relatives are enraged by what they see as portraits of themselves. In fact, Harry's life and writing are so intermingled that when his life is troubled by uncertainty his writing becomes indistinct.

For example, Robin Williams is Mel, a character in a screenplay by Harry. During the shooting of a scene in the movie Mel becomes blurred while the other characters remain in focus. The film technicians discover that the problem is not with the lenses or the camera but with Mel himself:

the implication is that the writer's indistinct conception of his character has caused the actor playing Mel to become blurred. So Harry is locked into a kind of binarism: he must use his life to clarify his writing and what thereby becomes clear is seen by his friends and family as personally insulting. But even when Harry presents his characters in a positive light he has problems living with the results. The second great scene in the movie takes place in hell, with Billy Crystal playing Satan. Harry journeys down to rescue Fay, his ex-girlfriend, from Satan. Instead, he comes upon his father who, according to Satan, is there because of his mistreatment of his son. Harry forgives his father and sends him off to a Chinese restaurant. Then Harry and Satan have a witty conversation in an air-conditioned cavern where they reminisce about their sexual conquests on earth. Harry again victimizes himself by explaining to Satan that he believes he can prevail against him because he is an even greater sinner than the fallen angel.

Finally, Harry attempts to redeem himself by taking his son to his old university where he is to receive recognition as a writer. However, since he has not been given permission by his ex-wife to take the son, he is eventually arrested for kidnapping. Nevertheless, the university hosts a party for him where we see the audience made up of the characters in the movie, suggesting that Harry's real friends are the characters of his creations. In the end, Harry finally grasps the idea of a writer whose only happiness is in his writing, and he begins to write a story about such a character, essentially the story of the movie. We are left at the conclusion with the ethical question: what should a man do whose successful writing is the result of his miserable life, his failure even when he attempts to do the decent thing? The question itself points beyond deconstruction, but in so far as the film ends there, it demonstrates the limitation of deconstruction and is, in that sense, aptly called "Deconstructing Harry."

The last film of this chapter illustrates how satirical humor applied to the self can achieve an ethical goal. Barry Levinson's "Man of the Year" (2006) stars Robin Williams as Tom Dobbs, a talk show host modeled after Steven Colbert or Jon Stewart. In one of the satirical sketches a member of the audience suggests that Dobbs should run for president, and, perhaps in order to carry on with the joke, he decides to run. The turning point in the movie is when Dobbs discovers that if he behaves like the other candidates in the contest he will have no chance of being noticed, let alone winning. Once he returns to his satirical, comical persona he surges in the polls. The process here is important. Because he has raised key issues, Dobbs is chosen to debate against the two frontrunners. During the debate, he interrupts the other candidate, breaks all the rules of decorum, and challenges his opponents in a comical way with devastating questions that leave them speechless and cause pandemonium on stage. Afterwards, Dobbs first believes that he has made a colossal mistake, but then he watches a replay of the debate and decides that he was acting in character and that his satirical humor led to his catching the attention of the audience who then listened to his views. Dobbs here deconstructs himself by way of humor: he remarks upon watching the replay that at first, before he got into his stride, he looked just like the others, a suit not a person. From this point onward, Dobbs distinguishes himself from the other candidates by his irony about himself as well as the others and by his undiplomatic answers: at one point, when the press is asking personal questions, he tells them that his right hand is stronger from masturbation and that he just farted. By this means, he shows that he is not pompous, does not take himself too seriously and wants to concentrate on the issues: in particular on the fact that the other candidates are far ahead in the polls because of all their money coming from wealthy individuals and companies who will expect payback. Although no one thinks that he has a chance of winning, the commentators admit that he is shaking up the system, exposing the fact that most viable candidates are beholden to special interest contributors. The poor and the needy, as Dobbs points out, are therefore neglected because they are without influence. Dobbs' humor decenters the election from personalities to the question of what is the effect of money on American elections.

Not surprisingly, as the election approaches it becomes clear that he has no real chance of making much of a showing, but there is a problem with the voting machines and, by way of an accident and a miscalculation, he is declared the winner. Eleanor, a woman who works for the voting machine company, tries to warn the proprietor of the company about this problem, but he decides to cover it up. In fact, to protect himself against Eleanor's claim he invents an originary myth to explain her outlandish accusation: she is a druggy with a long-term psychological problem. What eventually emerges is the truth: she has never taken drugs. In fact, employees of the company forcefully injected her with drugs to sedate her during the election. However, Eleanor, with the help of Dobbs, outwits the company by deconstructing their computer program and demonstrating that the problem involves alphabetical misreading.

Finally Dobbs decides to tell the truth to the electorate, walking away from the presidency. When asked whether he would like to run in the new election, he replies that he prefers to be a comedian on the sidelines who "shakes things up." Ironically, he is rewarded for his personal integrity. He is reportedly about to be tapped by *Time Magazine* as "Man of the Year" and his ratings as a comedian go sky high. A sharp contrast is set up between the head of the voting machine company and Dobbs. Eleanor's boss tries to bribe her, threatens her, fires her, and then sends someone to kill her. He will do whatever it takes to cover up his company's error. Dobbs, on the other hand, decides that he does not want to be president under false circumstances. The ability to see oneself from the point of view of the other, a phenomenon we first saw in Hans Lander of "Inglourious Basterds," is a hallmark of deconstruction.

"Man of the Year" ends with the suggestion that, in refusing to be a false president, Dobbs is a more important or a better person than the president. The "duly elected president" seems little different from other politicians. Once again, deconstruction shakes up and decenters the system, but none of the powers-that-be are overturned. The electoral process is perhaps slightly altered but only perhaps. Maybe the voting machines will work properly next time, but they may equally well malfunction again, and the truth may never be exposed. "Man of the Year" simply suggests that for some people individual integrity is worth the political sacrifice and for others it is not. Deconstruction opens the door for individual integrity; individual filmmakers decide how to use the opening in the seam of received opinion.

Conclusion: Films use deconstruction for ethical ends

All the movies in this chapter suggest how deconstruction can be used to arrive at the possibility of ethical choices, practical decisions made by individuals typified by that of Aldo Raine telling Lander that the thought of the SS officer shedding his uniform after the war is something "that I can't abide." Because these movies strive toward ethical not deconstructive final goals, they can be used to illustrate deconstruction but show no awareness—with the exception of "Deconstructing Harry" where ethics is indistinct—of this concept. The films use deconstruction as a means toward their own ends, and in those terms they serve two purposes: 1) to understand deconstruction; 2) to suggest how deconstruction is a useful strategy for discovering everyday, practical opportunities for ethical choices like those of Raine, Bourne, and Dobbs. While we pursue in subsequent chapters the theoretical ramifications of this concept, it is important to keep in mind that it, like all of the other theories presented in this volume, can also apply to quotidian life decisions.

In the next five chapters I propose to show how deconstruction is used for theoretical and ethical purposes. The literary theorists in the next five chapters question traditional assumptions and dichotomous beliefs. Derrida's assertion that neither philosophy nor any other discipline can master deconstruction raises some important theoretical questions. The following chapter considers how Michel Foucault applies deconstruction to the traditional notions of reason, truth, and knowledge, concepts that are basic to the other theoreticians in this volume.

CHAPTER TWO

Michel Foucault and "power-knowledge"

Summary: This chapter begins by explaining the concepts of "discourse" and "author-function" by way of "Shakespeare in Love." Since discourse is markedly affected by discipline, the next section is devoted to discipline and "Slumdog Millionaire." The internalized rules and regulations of discipline or "panopticonism" are exemplified in "Black Swan." Because the assumption for all of the preceding notions is "power-knowledge," this idea is discussed in reference to "An Education." But power is not all-pervasive, as is demonstrated by Foucault's study of sexuality, illustrated in the two Bridget Jones films. The conclusion applies the concept of "ethics of government" to the protagonists of all the films in this chapter.

Michel Foucault's work is a deconstruction of knowledge or the pursuit of truth: he believes that the educational procedure involves not only logic and reason, but also practice, that is, confronting various forms of power. Foucault's analysis of practice has consequences not only for literary criticism but also for our everyday lives. This chapter will focus upon two of Foucault's main ideas, "author-function" and "power-knowledge," that he combined in the last decade of his life in a study of the history of sexuality.

"Author-function" in "Shakespeare in Love"

In the late 1960s when Derrida first became known in the United States, Foucault entered dramatically onto the scene by announcing the "death of the author." This assertion should not be confused with the old formalist position that authorial intentions are to be excluded from considerations of the work of art. Rather, he asserted something more radical. In place of the term author, Foucault suggested "author-function," a concept illustrated by the very popular and successful movie first released in 1998, "Shakespeare in Love," directed by John Madden, starring Joseph Fiennes and Gwyneth Paltrow.

This movie clearly falls into the category often called "faction," that is, a mixture of fact and fiction. Many of the people and incidents in the movie are historically accurate. Certainly the presentation of the London Renaissance theater and the situation of the playwright are in accord with what scholars have pieced together from documents of the period. But Shakespeare's love relationship and many other elements of the movie are fiction. "Shakespeare in Love" changes the historical William Shakespeare, about whom we know precious little—experts in the field often point out that the undisputed facts would take up little more than two pages of print—into an "author-function," a combination of facts and speculation based upon the present-day view of Shakespeare derived from his writings. Students who think the film is a biography need to be disabused: rather it is a vivid presentation of what Shakespeare means to us, how he functions in our culture as possibly the greatest playwright of all time.

The plot of the movie focuses on the writing and rehearsing of *Romeo and Juliet*. Shakespeare is portrayed as a Romeo, although from a lower social station. The woman who is cast for the part of Juliet, his "love," is in fact the most improbable historical element of the film because women were not allowed on the public stage at the time and Juliet comes from a wealthy, middle-class family very unlikely to be associated with the theater. Yet the Shakespeare of the film asserts, as if he were living in a modern democratic society, that there is nothing to prevent an upper-middle-class woman from loving and marrying a poor poet. The present-day audience is not troubled by this historical inaccuracy because Shakespeare has come to have a particular function in our society, one that derives, for the most part, from productions of his plays. And the movie itself concludes by suggesting that the factional Shakespeare is ultimately more important than the "real" Shakespeare.

This cinematic version of *Romeo and Juliet* does not conclude as tragedy even though the lovers do not marry. When near the end Juliet goes off to Virginia with an aristocratic husband she does not love, the movie concludes, not with the death of the protagonists, but with Juliet suggesting upon leaving that Shakespeare comply with the request of Queen Elizabeth for a comedy about a woman. Shakespeare decides to name his heroine Viola, which is appropriately the name of the woman who plays Juliet. Moreover, we recognize here the reference to one of Shakespeare's great comedies, so the conclusion is that Shakespeare as a factionalized author or "author-function" is more important for us than the personal dilemma of the author mourning the loss of his beloved. In that sense, the film concludes by suggesting the death of the author together with his personal problems concerning his love life and its replacement by the "author-function," the playwright of *Twelfth Night*. The film ends with the poor bereft poet using Juliet/Viola as a muse or inspiration for a new play, a comedy for the Twelfth Night festivities, as the Queen has suggested.

Nevertheless, the Queen has recognized that *Romeo and Juliet* is a just representation of love. In fact, she orders Lord Wessex to pay Shakespeare fifty pounds as the winner of the bet about whether a play can capture the nature of true love. Not only is she recognizing the power of Shakespeare's play but also that he and Juliet/Viola are in love. To Wessex she remarks that he is a fool because Juliet/Viola "has already been plucked." But even Elizabeth I does not have the power, as she herself points out, to override the marriage vows. And here we begin to see how the concept of "author-function" is related to Shakespeare's public and private life. In his garret before he meets Juliet/Viola he struggles to write with ink-stained nails and a quill but is without inspiration: he is hounded by the theatre managers to fulfill his contract as a poet, one element of his "author-function." Then in public with the Queen we see him being pressed to be a loyal subject and obey the laws of marriage, particularly since he is an important writer, ready to perform the social function of the author.

In this respect, "Shakespeare in Love" is once again pertinent in its presentation of "power-knowledge." The "author-function" is shown to develop from many different kinds of power: economic, social, psychological, and political. The film cleverly suggests that the problems that plague the relationship of Romeo and Juliet, personal, familial, societal, and cultural, are analogous to the powers that constrict Shakespeare as a playwright. And although Shakespeare was probably considered even in his own day one of, if not the greatest of playwrights, he was constantly harried by the authorities, from the actors and theater owners pressing for parts and new plays, to the Master of the Revels threatening to censure lines or close the theater. In fact, Shakespeare as playwright shows Juliet that he is an apt Romeo by negotiating these various obstacles, persuading the lead actor to play the part of Mercutio, convincing the theatre manager and owner that, although a tragedy, the play will be successful financially, and concealing for a time from the Master of the Revels that the part of Juliet is played by a woman.

In fact, Shakespeare is presented as a subversive. In addition to the risk of allowing a woman on stage, he asserts himself equal to an aristocratic rival in his love of Juliet and fights a duel with him, both of which constitute not only a breach of decorum, if not of the law, but also a questioning of the social class system which was at that time considered sacrosanct. Indeed, the film version of Shakespeare is that of a post-romantic writer who composes erratically in a garret, visits a herbalist/shrink, and leads a bohemian lifestyle. Again, historical inaccuracy is not important because the point is what Shakespeare is to us; the film is about our society, our perception of the relationship between art and forms of power that present obstacles to its realization.

Foucault formulates this position in the following way: "the function of an author is to characterize the existence, circulation, and operation of certain forces within a society" (*What is*, 142). The author has a function in a society, and that function is more important than what he or she may actually be in his or her inner being. Moreover the concept of author-function varies with historical periods. The example Foucault cites is in the context of science. In the middle ages the name of the scientist, rather than the content of his treatise, was the basis of confidence and authority. Medieval science could only gain credit by associating itself with the great names of the past, such as Paracelsus or Galen. Modern-day science is quite the reverse. The author is less important because authority derives mainly from the content or what scientists today call repeatability, the empirical test for all assertions made by scientists. Since the "author-function" changes with history, we are encouraged by Foucault to focus not upon the ego of the author but upon the discursive conditions of his or her creation.

> We should suspend the typical questions: how does a free subject penetrate the density of things and endow them with meaning: how does it accomplish its design by animating the rules of discourse from within? Rather, we should ask: under what conditions and through what forms can an entity like the subject appear in the order of the discourse: what position does it occupy; what function does it exhibit; and what rules does it follow in each type of discourse? In short, the subject [...] must be stripped of its creative role and analysed as a complex and variable function of discourse (*What is*, 148).

"Shakespeare in Love" illustrates this point when the Queen recognizes Shakespeare's genius by witnessing his play: she decides that he understands and can communicate love and therefore directs him to employ his talent, not in stealing an aristocrat's bride, but in writing a comedy about love. That Shakespeare may find this advice frustrating is of no concern to the Queen: rather, she is pointing to a function for Shakespeare in the socio-political world over which she reigns. But even Elizabeth I does not have complete control of this realm: Shakespeare may have found a place for himself at court, leading to recognition among the ruling class, but his plays must still make money, must also please the groundlings.

One of the social forces shared by Shakespeare in his day and "Shakespeare in Love" in ours is the profit motive. This film was commercially successful in part because it skillfully portrayed and played upon the "author-function" of Shakespeare in our time and took some license with the historical situation of Shakespeare. Accordingly, the film uses as a framing device the profit motive: it opens with the feet of the theater manager in the fire because he owes money to the "angel," the person who funds the play, and it ends with a standing ovation by a full house, a sign of financial success. Both the movie-maker and the playwright make a profit because they understand their place in the economic discourse of their respective eras: Shakespeare as the poet of the court and the entertainer of the groundlings, the movie-maker as one who makes the great Bard of love a man in love. But understanding discourse is complex:

> We should not imagine that the world presents us with a legible face, leaving us merely to decipher it; it does not work hand in glove with what we already know; there is no pre-discursive fate disposing the word in our favor. We must conceive discourse as a violence that we do to things, or, and at all events, as a practice we impose upon them; it is in this practice that the events of discourse find the principle of their regularity (*The Discourse*, 158)

Discourse for Foucault and the other theorists in this volume involves all forms of communication, from language and body language to visual signs and pictures as well as sounds, not only speech but also music and other aural occurrences—anything that functions in the transmission of information. And Foucault argues that none of these forms of communication are natural, easy, or readily available. On the contrary, they involve acquired skills and even then remain difficult. Shakespeare complains to his herbalist/shrink that he has writer's block. In the course of the film we see that the overcoming of this problem involves first finding a muse or inspiration, provided by Juliet/Viola, then help from colleagues like Kit Marlowe, and finally recognition of his art in the form of ticket sales, applause from the audience, and praise from the Queen, critics, and others in his profession. This difficult process, and it is a struggle even for Shakespeare, makes the great Bard human, a genius of course but one of us. The implication is that the concepts of "author-function" and "discourse" apply beyond the bounds of literature: the cultural forces that transform the "author" into an "author-function" affect each of us in our daily lives as we fulfill our routine functions: we are subject to the same kinds of social forces that effect Shakespeare as a present-day "author-function," if not as authors, then as parents or children, workers or bosses, etc.

For Foucault, we need to understand these forces that result in the practice of doing "violence" to things by way of a form of discourse that he calls "disciplines." This term can be understood as referring to the names of the departments of the university: botany, history, psychology, that is, the various fields of knowledge: "We tend to see [...] disciplines [as] so many infinite resources available for the creation of discourse. Perhaps so, but they are nonetheless principles of constraint; and it is probably impossible to appreciate their positive, multiplicatory role without first taking into consideration their restrictive, constraining role" (*The Discourse*, 155). Foucault's point is that the disciplines of knowledge limit our discourse, restricting how we speak and write. The historian, for example, is not supposed to treat the facts of history as if they were fiction, that is, to apply the discipline of literature or literary criticism to facts or real events. Similarly the botanist, in his professional role, does not describe the structure of a plant in psychological terms as if it were a person. We take these differences between the disciplines to be a matter of common sense, but Foucault insists they are arbitrary constraints. We are made aware of this unnatural element of discourse when we find ourselves fulfilling functions we had not anticipated, as when Shakespeare, having broken the law prohibiting women on the stage, is directed by the Queen to write a comedy for the Twelfth Night festivities. And although the Queen formulates her desire as a suggestion, Shakespeare knows full well it is a command, a requirement of his discipline as a playwright.

Discipline in "Slumdog Millionaire"

"Slumdog Millionaire" (2008), directed by Danny Boyle, starring Dev Patel as Jamal, is a fine example of the restraints power places upon knowledge and the discipline necessary to gain and impart knowledge. The formal structure of the movie makes plain that discipline is its subject: we see a young man, Jamal, being asked questions on a television quiz show juxtaposed with his being tortured in a police station. Such behavior recalls Foucault's title for his work on this topic, *Discipline and Punish*. Of course, Foucault knows that only in extreme circumstances is the punishment a form of torture, but we are all subject to punishment in the quest for knowledge, thwarted by power in the form of arbitrary requirements about the form and structure of "truth," from grammar and spelling rules to the conventions of any particular discipline. The function of this juxtaposition is to show how Jamal's acceptance of punishment and disciplined intelligent response leads him to the knowledge necessary to answer the questions on the quiz program. After each question is posed, the movie takes us to an event in the contestant's life that helps explain how he is able to answer the question. After the young man has won a large sum of money, the master of ceremonies, suspecting cheating, turns him over to the police who interrogate and torture him. The film proceeds by adroitly showing us the truth of what the young man claims to the police, that all of his answers derive from what he has learned from his life as a slumdog. And the constraints imposed by power with regard to the discipline of acquiring and imparting knowledge are no less obvious in the slum than on a quiz show.

The film is cleverly structured so that the audience learns as onlookers what the police inspector finally grudgingly accepts: the assumption that a slumdog could not have gained sufficient knowledge to answer the quiz show questions is erroneous. His knowledge comes from escaping or negotiating with forms of power, that is, his physical and mental agility. He runs from the religious bigots who kill his mother and the hoodlum who tries to blind him, discovers where Latika is being kept and outmaneuvers the gangster who has captured her. And of course the very first and most vivid event for the main character is when as a young child he is locked in the outhouse and can only escape by going down the toilet through the sewage pipes. Covered in sewage, he emerges extending his filthy hand with a piece of paper to receive the autograph of the latest pop idol who probably emerged from a similar environment. Even at this early stage of his life, discipline and punishment are both manifest. Like the discipline displayed in his insistent search for Latika, Jamal focuses on the only means of getting the autograph, submitting to the ordeal of the sewage.

The police inspector comes to realize that Jamal's answers correspond to episodes in his life; we learn that, for a slumdog to survive, he or she must learn how to endure extreme hardship and understand how to evade or negotiate with the powers-that-be. Finally, as a millionaire, Jamal will be giving his autograph rather than receiving one, suggesting that this slum does not explode into revolution because most of the inhabitants dream of being a pop star or a millionaire. And here we see why Foucault views power as forming the base of discourse, in this instance, that of television. When Jamal is on the threshold of winning the jackpot, the whole of India is watching the show along with all the other slumdogs rooting for him. And at that moment he becomes the rival of the master of ceremonies, himself a slumdog of the past, which leads us to the climactic moment, the answer to the next-to-last question. The slumdog has been told by the master of ceremonies the letter that corresponds to what supposedly is the correct answer. But, when in front of the camera, even though he admits that he does not know the answer, Jamal decides not to choose the answer to the question offered by the man who should know. Why? Because for his entire life Jamal has dealt with people in positions of power over him, most recently his brother, a drug dealer who has helped steal the woman he has adored since early childhood. Moreover, since the master of ceremonies referred to his previous life in the slums, Jamal knows that he too has struggled through the sewage of life to get to his position. Jamal recognizes that it is very unlikely that a slumdog—whether it be his brother or the master of ceremonies—who has struck gold would be willing to share such a prize with another slumdog. He therefore eliminates the answer given him by the master of ceremonies. But at the same time he only gets back his beloved after she has been exploited and abused and marked, literally scarred, by her past as a prostitute. "Slumdog Millionaire" provides the audience with the knowledge of the Mumbai slums: even those who survive and achieve stardom, from the master of ceremonies to Jamal, never lose the scars of the slum. Indeed, their achievements result in part from their knowledge of this fact.

The film concludes with a Bollywood-style dance on the station platform celebrating the love of Jamal, now a millionaire, and Latika. But while Jamal is winning the jackpot, his older brother Salim dies in a bathtub full of money. Although Salim saved Jamal from being blinded, Jamal cannot forgive him for selling Latika into prostitution. So Salim shoots his gangster boss, Latika's pimp, and lies in the tub of money as the other gang members kill him The two brothers have pursued very different paths. Salim goes for the money as a hired gun and lies to his brother about Latika. Jamal remains straight and truthful, finally rejecting his brother for betraying Latika. Indeed, the police inspector, after completing his interrogation of Jamal, points out that never before has he encountered a case when the accusation of fraud, that is, cheating on the quiz show, is averted by implication in a murder. For Jamal confesses that he learned one of the answers to a quiz show question by witnessing his brother use a Colt revolver to kill the leader of the beggars. The police inspector concludes that Jamal does not lie but tells the truth too much. Jamal's quest for truth and love is also marked by decency; upon finding one of the children who was blinded by the leader of the beggars, Jamal gives him a $100 bill. The blind boy verifies the amount by asking whose picture is on the bill; Benjamin Franklin is the answer to a question put to Jamal on the television program.

The difference between the two brothers is key to the resolution of the film. Jamal goes for the jackpot, not for the money but to free Latika, and so he is committed to using his wits to evade the obstacles of power. Salim uses a gun against power and ends with money but cannot live with being rejected by his brother: Salim did not realize that he needed the love and respect of Jamal until it was too late. Salim confronted power with power, which became an end in itself, not a means to learn by way of discipline. For Jamal, by contrast, power is a means to knowledge, both of which are needed to regain Latika.

We need to distinguish between confrontation with power, Salim's natural aggression, and the understanding and negotiation with power, the strategy of Jamal. In this regard, Foucault refers to Jeremy Bentham's

Panopticon. In the late nineteenth century, Bentham designed a new sort of prison: an architectural plan intended to be built, not simply an illustration of a theory, that is, in Foucault's terms, not only words but also practice or behavior. The principle of this design was that of a kind of glass pyramid with one central guard at the top able to see into the individual cells of all the prisoners who were themselves isolated, unable to see one another or to see the guard above them. The result was that because the prisoners never knew whether the guard was there or not they ultimately became their own guards.

For Foucault this structure symbolizes the internalization or acceptance of power so that the experience for the individual prisoner—and we are all prisoners of society in one form or another—is that we feel self-motivated or experience what Foucault calls "the will to knowledge." "Panopticonism is the general principle of the new 'political anatomy' whose object and end are not the relation of sovereignty but the relation of 'discipline'." The result of this new kind of power is, according to Foucault, that "persons resemble factories and schools, barracks, hospitals which all resemble persons" (*Discipline and Punish*, 228). The point is that the uniform behavior (literally and figuratively) of school children, soldiers, and factory workers is not different in kind from all people who speak, dress, and act in accord with codes and mores that they have internalized, that is, think of as "natural."

Panopticonism and "Black Swan"

"Black Swan," directed by Darren Aronofsky and starring Natalie Portman and Vincent Cassel, first appeared in 2010. The film is about the presentation of a version of "Swan Lake" which pits an innocent, virginal white swan against a sensual, evil black swan. Nina, the protagonist, played by Natalie Portman, auditions for the part, but the director, Thomas Leroy, played by Vincent Cassel, tells her that she is perfect as the white swan but too prim and proper for the black swan. Thomas advises Nina to gain passion by throwing herself into the role.

First Nina works on her technique, but the director during a rehearsal of a pas de deux asks Nina's partner would he want to "fuck" her. Later Thomas explains that Lily, Nina's rival for the part, has all the qualities needed for the part of the black swan, and we subsequently learn that Lily is having an affair with the male lead. In an attempt to loosen Nina up, Thomas kisses her passionately and she bites him. As a result of this sign of Nina's passion Thomas reconsiders whether to assign her the part. Immediately after this episode, Nina goes home, where we discover that her mother is trying to stop Nina from harming herself. The tendency toward self-punishment becomes more pronounced as Nina competes against Lily. Nina begins to have hallucinations; in particular, that she has had sex with Lily. So consumed is Nina with her illusion of a sexual liaison with her rival that she confronts her about it, only to be told that on the night in question Lily was with her boyfriend.

But the hallucinations continue until we reach the climactic scene in Nina's dressing room during the interval of a performance of the ballet. Nina has finished the first act as the white swan. During the final jump she had an hallucination of Lily and her boyfriend offstage having sex. As a result, she loses concentration and is dropped by her partner, but when asked by the director for an explanation she blames her partner. We see the first glimpse of the emerging black swan. She then returns to her dressing room where in front of her mirror she sees, or believes that she sees, Lily as the black swan explaining that she will dance the rest of the ballet. In her struggle with what the mirror now shows as her double, Nina breaks the mirror using a shard to murder Lily. She then dances brilliantly, receives a standing ovation and ends her performance exclaiming, "I felt it. Perfect. It was perfect." But it soon becomes clear that Nina has in fact stabbed herself; the killing of Lily was a figment of her imagination.

At this point the audience is surprised, since we too have been deceived: the murder of Lily appeared to be real. In short, the director wants us to believe that Nina, the prim and proper white swan, has developed into a woman capable of murder, a black swan. The potential for passion Thomas recognized in her bite/kiss has been realized: the procedure involves panopticonism. At first, Nina is the prisoner of others, the director, her mother, and her rival. But in her disciplined desire to be awarded the part and perform it to her utmost, she internalizes these others and what they require of her. In fact, her rival Lily becomes her double. The mother whom she has defied is in the audience with tears of love and appreciation. And after the ballet Nina kisses Thomas so passionately that he is literally "gob-smacked." She has become her own director, mother, and rival. Lying bleeding with a wound that may be fatal, but ecstatically feeling for the first time "perfection," Nina must now realize that the forces that drove her to perform so brilliantly came from within.

Foucault calls this sort of awareness "power-knowledge," which is distinguished from the fruits of logic and reason that are conceptual and cerebral. "Power-knowledge," by contrast, is physically experienced in the body, not merely thinking alone but also acting. We often separate our scrapes with authority during our education from our academic achievement, our knowledge, but Foucault suggests that the two are intimately bound together; coping with the rules and regulations of school and university, the local powers-that-be, affects education, which together with the mental element constitutes "power-knowledge."

Power-knowledge: "An Education"

An excellent example of how this kind of knowledge is distinguished from rational cognition can be seen in "An Education" (2009), directed by Lone Scherfig, starring Carey Mulligan as Jenny Miller. In the 1960s, Jenny, an intelligent and promising student in her last year of school, has hopes of being admitted to Oxford. But she meets David Goldman, a man in his late twenties, who lives a high life and shows her an alternative to the dull routine of the suburbs she has endured all her life. Then David sets about charming Jenny's family, and the couple become engaged, leading to her dropping out of school to get married.

But just before the marriage and after Jenny and David have been seen in public as an engaged couple and traveled abroad together, Jenny discovers in the glove compartment of David's very luxurious car letters addressed to him from his wife. It turns out that David is a married con man who has deceived other women but now seems genuinely in love with Jenny. Eventually Jenny breaks away from him and attempts to return to school. At this point in the movie we see most overtly the concept of power—manifested as punishment—and its relationship to knowledge. Jenny goes to the head mistress, played by Emma Thomson, who refuses to allow her back in school mainly because she is a bad role model for the other girls. This decision has nothing whatever to do with Jenny's academic intelligence or ability to complete the subjects necessary to get into university.

Power-knowledge is seen earlier in the film. David persuades Jenny's parents that his taking her to Oxford will be advantageous to her because he knows C. S. Lewis and will introduce Jenny to him. After a luxurious weekend with David's friends, Danny and Helen, Jenny witnesses David forging a note and signature in a book written by Lewis that she gives to her parents as evidence of her meeting with the famous author. Jenny goes along with this fiction, probably realizing that her independence from her very protective parents or parental power will require some deception.

The second example of "power knowledge," however, causes Jenny more pangs of conscience. She and Helen are told to wait in the car while David and Danny go into an old woman's house and emerge in a great hurry with an antique map. Jenny, we assume, is upset at being peremptorily ordered to wait and seems aware that the original owner of the map has been taken advantage of. But David placates her by explaining that he and Danny are in the business of acquiring such objects that, he asserts, are better appreciated by his clients. Also, he adds, we bring poor and black people into neighborhoods of old people who then panic and sell their property cheaply to David and Danny. Jenny is finally convinced when David uses the same metaphor that her father used; money does not grow in trees. The high life that we live and you enjoy comes at a price. Since we, David continues, do not have academic intelligence we have learned how to make our way commercially. It is somewhat risky, he implies, but involves high rewards of the sort Jenny enjoys. Power-knowledge here involves those excluded from the establishment, symbolized by David as a Jew. David's luxurious lifestyle involves business ventures that exploit others, but the only alternative for Jenny is the boring penny-pinching world of her parents. Jenny is coming to understand the entrepreneurial skills necessary for people who have desires above their socio-economic class. And class is, of course, a form of power, of a subtle, insidious sort.

Her final and most important confrontation with power involves, as the title of the film indicates, education, which in this case actually prevents education, at least until Jenny finds an alternative to formal schooling. She has befriended one of the teachers at the school, who agrees to tutor and help her with preparation for the exams, which she then passes. The education of Jenny involves negotiation with kinds of pedagogic power that have nothing to do with intellectual or academic challenges.

Similarly, David is educated by Jenny's rejection of him; prior to that moment he has been able to charm most people and devise ways of acquiring the money to buy whatever he wants. Now he is rejected by possibly the only woman he has ever loved. Ironically, he has given her the self-confidence that enables her to reject him. Jenny has panopticonized David's belief in himself/herself and his ability to get what s(he) wants. The sexual scenes between David and Jenny are where we see this new development, Jenny seeing herself as attractive and worthy in her own right and David becoming enamored with the woman emerging from the girl. In the scene where Jenny loses her virginity, she insists that she and David cease using childish names for one another and treat each other like adults. Indeed, she becomes a source of power-knowledge to be conveyed to David. He offers a banana to get over "the messy stuff" and she refuses to continue, bringing him to awareness of his insensitivity.

Once Jenny learns that David is married, however, she turns away from the life of entrepreneurial luxury to that of academic discipline. Why? Most probably out of recognition that she has the intellectual ability to pursue something other than David's shady kind of business. The obstacle now takes the form of the power of the headmistress, whose refusal to have Jenny back seems to further motivate her to go to university. She learns from rejection how important it is to be a part of the respectable establishment, and so she goes to Oxford and puts her relationship with David behind her. At the end of the movie, Jenny tells us while riding her bike at university that she sees a number of the young men whom Helen, the girl friend of David's friend, warned would be immature and "spotty." In fact, one of them has invited her to Paris, where David had earlier taken her, and she tells the young man that she would love to go, as if she had never been there. Jenny's education involves not merely entrance to Oxford but also panopticonizing the conventions, mores, and morality of the educated undergraduate. She has internalized the discipline of studentship by first violating some of those mores and being punished by her head mistress. Discipline and punishment are the means power uses to educate, to impart "power-knowledge," and Foucault goes on in the final phase of his career to analyze sexuality, what Jenny discovers about herself in the bedroom with David. The lesson for us is that education or knowledge are not merely thinking but involve strategic actions with regard to dangerous and powerful forces: no ivory tower can escape the powers of "power-knowledge." But it would be a mistake to assume that for Foucault life is only a struggle with power; we each have an inner sanctum of limited scope that is not completely controlled by others, and that is the realm of sexuality.

In the last decade of his life Foucault turned to the history of sexuality in a three-volume work that appeared during the 1970s and early 1980s. Sexuality became an interest because, given the many constraints of the disciplines of knowledge, it was seen as a means of some personal freedom and the source of the will to or drive for knowledge. The study of sexuality begins by pointing out that the general assumption that sex has been repressed in the Victorian period and in our society involves a misunderstanding. "One could plot a line going straight from the seventeenth-century pastoral to what became its projection in literature, 'scandalous' literature at that. 'Tell everything,' the directors would say time and again: 'not only consummated acts but sensual touchings, all impure gazes, all obscene remarks [...] all consenting thoughts" (History, 1, 21). Instead of repression we are encouraged to confess, if not our sins to the priest, then our libidinous thoughts to our shrinks and confidants. Foucault continues: "we have not only witnessed an explosion of unorthodox sexualities but—and this is the important point—a deployment quite different from the law, even if it is locally dependent on procedures of prohibition, has ensured through a network of interconnecting mechanisms the proliferation of specific pleasures and the multiplication of disparate sexualities" (History, 1, 49). So Foucault's method is, not to note the means of repression, but to begin with the mechanisms that "produce knowledge multiplied by discourse that induced pleasure and generated power." In short, Foucault suggests that the object of his study is "to understand how our obsession with sexuality is related to the will to power. As far as sexuality is concerned, we shall attempt to constitute the 'political economy' of a will to knowledge" (History, 1, 73).

The discipline of sexuality: Bridget Jones

A fine example of the relationship between power, knowledge, and discipline in the context of sexuality is provided by the recent "Bridget Jones" movies, the first of which dates from 2001 and the sequel, 2004, both directed by Sharon Maguire and starring Renée Zellweger. These movies are presented as diaries, that is, as confessionals narrated by Bridget. We are given access to her most intimate thoughts, a large proportion of which relate to sex and sexuality. Indeed, she decides to keep a diary in order to improve her love life, and at the end of Part One she is given a new diary so that she may make a fresh start with a new love relationship. Foucault explains our interest in sex in the following terms:

> Among its many emblems, our society wears that of the talking sex. The sex which one catches unawares and questions, and which, restrained and loquacious at the same time, endlessly replies [...]. As if it were essential for us to be able to draw from that little piece of ourselves not only pleasure but also knowledge, and a whole subtle interchange from one to the other: a knowledge of pleasure, a pleasure that comes of knowing pleasure, a knowledge-pleasure; and as if that fantastic animal had itself such finely tuned ears, such searching eyes, so gifted a tongue and mind, as to know much and be quite willing to tell it, provided we employed a little skill in urging it to speak (*History*, 1, 77).

The diary is a perfect ruse for talking sex, a genre that permits intimate thoughts without, in Foucault's terms, having to be urged to speak. Bridget's love life involves two men: Daniel Cleaver, played by Hugh Grant, a womanizer, handsome and charming but totally unscrupulous, and Mark Darcy, played by Colin Firth, a strait-laced barrister who is uptight but decent and trustworthy. Bridget begins her diary with the sorts of axioms typical of a discipline, what not to do, or, in this instance, the sort of person to avoid: "alcoholic, workaholic, peeping-tom, megalo-maniac, emotional fuckwit and a pervert." Sexuality for Bridget is her form of personal expression, perhaps the only time she can say what she likes, an illusion that is shattered at the end of Part One when Mark reads her diary and, she believes, leaves her forever. For, as Foucault points out, no discipline is without restrictions; even a diary cannot be taken to be absolute truth. "What has been, what still is [...] this will to truth which has survived throughout so many centuries of our history [...] is a system of exclusion" (*The Discourse*, 150). The belief that in any situation one can speak the truth or just what you wish to say at the moment is naïve and subject to what Foucault calls punishment, something Bridget experi-ences regularly.

By contrast, Mark is discreet and disciplined, yet at the end Bridget hopes to marry him. In Part One, Bridget tells us in her frank and off-hand manner that she is attracted to the candor and casual style of Daniel, aptly illustrated by his remark to her: "I like your tits in that top." Mark, on the other hand, she finds standoffish and arrogant, particularly when she overhears him referring to her conversation as "verbal incontinence." In Part One, Bridget eventually learns that Daniel is disloyal to his friends and lovers and that Mark, however reserved, is more dependable. The key event in Part One is Mark's successful defense of a Kurdish freedom fighter and his wife who are granted asylum in Great Britain rather than face the possibility of torture and even death in their homeland. At the core of this comedy about the mores of courtship or, more accurately in present-day or Foucauldian terms, the conventions of sexuality, is the very real threat of punishment. Moreover, it is in this scene that Mark first acts to demonstrate his attraction to Bridget by arranging for her to have an exclusive interview with his client, an event that makes Bridget into a major figure as a television journalist. Bridget's rise to television prominence is the result of Mark's discipline. He alone decides to keep the other journalists away from his client and therefore can provide exclusive coverage to Bridget.

Bridget learns that courtship without rules can only lead to short-term affairs, not marriage. At the end of the first movie, Bridget, in a snow storm, half undressed, kisses Mark fully dressed in a suit and overcoat holding a new diary, and we are left with the hopeful but farcical image of two lovers as different from one another as their attire. What draws them together is difference. Immaculate, discreet, Mark is attracted to Bridget, the scruffy screw-up who regularly makes a fool of herself. Bridget seeks the passion buried in this repressed barrister. In terms of the conventions of sexuality, the discipline of courtship, the question is whether the couple can find a way to accommodate the spontaneity of Bridget and the self-control of Mark. But the process of courtship is discipline by way of exclusions. Bridget insists that Mark be less arrogant and snobby, more forthcoming with his feelings, and stop wearing the hideous sweaters given to him by his mother at Christmas. Mark teaches Bridget discretion, trust, and the value of silence. Once they each accept these and other requirements of one another, they can begin to discover deeper elements or the "truth" about one another.

But Foucault insists that the truth-seeking process excludes monsters like Mark in his Christmas sweater or Bridget applying cosmetics so that she looks like a clown. In the context of science, Foucault explains:

Within its own limits, every discipline recognises true and false propositions, but it repulses a whole teratology of learning. The exterior of a science is both more, and less, populated than one might think [...] there are no errors in the strict sense of the term, for error can only emerge and be identified within a well defined process; there are monsters on the prowl, however, whose forms alter with the history of knowledge. In short, a proposition must fulfill some onerous and complex conditions before it can be admitted within a discipline; before it can be pronounced true or false, it must be [...] "within the true" (*The Discourse*, 154).

For example, once Bridget discovers that Daniel has been unfaithful to her he never falls within the true. In a moment of weakness, plied with many drinks, she nearly succumbs a second time to his charms. But, in general, in contrast to her attitude to Mark, she makes no courtship demands on Daniel, whom she regards as a seducer; in Foucault's terms, a monster on the prowl.

By the beginning of Part Two, "Bridget Jones: The Edge of Reason," Bridget and Mark are an item, and the development of their relationship concerns Bridget's release from prison in Thailand, again suggestive of Foucault's *Discipline and Punish*. In this regard it is important to remember that both films contain a fistfight between Daniel and Mark, the second of which ends with one of the great lines of the movies. Taunting Mark, Daniel quips "if you are so concerned about Bridget you should marry her and then certainly 'she'll shag me'." The cad has the last witty word, but Mark wins Bridget in the end because he does not flout the conventions of decency and courtship. Of course, Bridget is punished for breaking the rules. Although comically presented, Bridget's time in prison is difficult, particularly as there seems to be no hope of early release. Moreover, what Bridget learns from her fellow prisoners—women abused by men for sexual purposes—is that the constrictions of courtship in England are a mild version of the harsh realities faced by exploited women in Thailand.

Even before prison, Bridget is continually breaking the rules of courtship, either because her conversation is too inane for Mark or because she is too forward with Daniel in assuming they are an item. And, lest we dismiss these issues as punctilio, mere manners, they are part of the reason for the two fistfights between Daniel and Mark. The main issue in the first fight is that Daniel went to bed with the woman who was at that time Mark's wife and lied to Bridget, telling her instead that Mark had an affair with Daniel's fiancée. In the sequel Mark attacks Daniel for leaving Bridget on her own to cope with the Thai police when she only visited the country at Daniel's insistent invitation.

The significance of the rules or mores of courtship is most prominent in the scene in the sequel when Bridget is invited by Mark to attend a formal party at the Inns of Court. Having gone to a great deal of trouble to find the appropriate dress and cosmetics she arrives soaking wet in unsuitable attire, her face a mess. She begins a conversation with the guests—investors, lawyers and judges—who are Mark's associates and clients. The topic is charity. The two legal professionals, clearly successful and well off, hold the view that there is no need for charity because those who have lost their home and assets are themselves responsible and should not expect help from others. Bridget disagrees, gains no ground in the argument, and loses her temper, finally calling them "stupid Tory cunts." Having insulted Mark's business associates, she apologizes to Mark even though continuing to believe what she said is right. So the conventions and mores of the work-a-day world are directly related to those of sexuality and marriage. Even though Mark agrees with Bridget's views on charity, he feels that as an act of respect to him she should have held her tongue with his colleagues.

Moreover, Mark's response to Bridget's social gaffes is directly related to his expression of sexuality and to his personal development, a key factor in Foucault's argument. Mark Darcy's name is a clear reference to Mr. Darcy, a part Colin Firth played in the BBC adaptation of Jane Austen's *Pride and Prejudice.* Both characters share an external reserve that covers a smoldering passion, an element that becomes clear at the resolution of "The Edge of Reason," a title which is perhaps an indirect reference to Jane Austen, whose novels first appeared in print at the end of a period often referred to as "The Age of Reason." Once again, the paradoxical nature of the relationship is manifest: Mark is simultaneously drawn to and repelled by the blunt tactlessness of Bridget, and she has similarly conflicted views of his cold self-control. The question posed by Part Two is a Foucauldian one: will the constraints of sexuality permit sufficient personal freedom for these two people to be happily married to one another?

When Mark arrives at the prison to announce to Bridget that she is to be released, he presents himself as a distant professional. When Bridget thanks him, he professes to be the mere messenger of higher authorities and to have no interest in her circumstances, particularly her relationship with Daniel. We are led to share Bridget's assumption that he no longer cares for her. But Bridget's friends subsequently explain to her that Mark has gone to immense effort and used great influence and expertise, money, and time to effect her release. Ironically, Mark's uptight Tory background serves him well in this context because it provides the contacts necessary for her release. Moreover, not only has he exhibited total dedication to freeing her, but he also bears a personal grudge against Daniel for deserting her at a time of urgent need. Mark's rigid code of ethics makes him a loyal friend but an unimaginative lover. Indeed, the movie ends with Bridget teaching Mark how to propose to her, that is, once she understands that he loves her "just as she is," she provides him with the discourse of a marriage proposal. This scene is literally a double-take. During the first take, Bridget interrupts Mark who is thereby put off, unable to proceed, explaining that the moment is gone. But Bridget insists on a retake, this time without interruption. While she is coaching Mark into expressing his emotion, she is herself learning discretion, even how at key moments to be silent. We return to the "author-function," specifically a "diarist-function" since Bridget learns discretion as a diarist while Mark might be described as learning his "lover-function" in the double-take scene. Sexuality becomes for Foucault a means of self-expression, albeit limited, within the confines of discourse-controlled social functions.

The subplot in Part Two concerning Bridget's parents' temporary breakup reinforces this point. Bridget's mother finds an equivalent of Daniel in his capacity as the "smooth guide" on a television travel show. Julian, a suave television presenter, turns out to be petty and unkind. Eventually, Bridget's mother returns to her husband, who resembles Mark in being less flamboyant and colorful (literally) but who is disciplined and reliable. This character element we have seen at the Christmas parties that Bridget's father endures stoically, even though, as he admits to his daughter, for him they are living death. Now Bridget's mother asks of her husband, as her daughter does of Mark, that he be more demonstrative in his affection for her. The marriage at the end of the movie is not that of Bridget and Mark but the remarriage of her parents, suggesting that sexuality is a concern throughout present-day society involving people of all ages. As Bridget remarks, in her characteristically indiscreet terms, "I am still not married and my 'fucking parents' are marrying one another a second time." In a society fraught with so many constricting disciplines that define our "functions," sexuality provides a partial means of self-expression. Pertinent in this respect is the revelation near the end of Part Two that Rebecca, the woman Bridget took to be her rival for Mark's affection, is in fact a lesbian. Foucault comments on homosexuality in the following terms:

> Nineteenth century "bourgeois" society—and it is less doubtless still with us—was a society of blatant and fragmented perversion. And this was not by way of hypocrisy, for nothing was more manifest and more prolix, or more manifestly taken over by discourses and institutions. [...] At issue, rather, is the type of power it brought to bear upon the body and on sex [...] it acted by multiplication of singular sexualities. It did not set boundaries for sexuality, but included it in the body as a mode of specification for individuals. [...] It produced and determined the sexual mosaic. Modern society is perverse, not in spite of its Puritanism or as if from a backlash provoked by its hypocrisy; it is in actual fact, perverse (*History*, 1, 47).

Perversity here refers to our obsession with sexuality as a means of differentiating among ourselves, a means toward individuation. The recent focus on the topic of homosexual marriage, its entry into legal discourse, is another indication that sexuality is fast becoming a major form of self-expression.

For literary theory the message is clear. The literary critic must understand the rules of the discipline, the "critic function," in order to communicate knowledge about literature. These constraints will be different from those of other disciplines and will be subject to historical change. But beyond the application to critics and criticism, a more general point can be made. Sexuality is an area of self-expression in a society marked by ever-increasing areas of discipline and punishment: whatever limited freedom is allotted to us is dependent upon our understanding of the constraints imposed upon us by disciplines which limit our choices, even those concerning such personal matters as sexuality. And here Foucault is led, near the end of his life, to turn to the ethics of the government of the individual, by which he means the state regulation of individual liberty.

Foucault on the ethics of individual government

In an essay first published in 1983, a year before his death, Foucault summarized his work for the past 20 years. The title of this essay is "Why Study Power: the Question of the Subject." Foucault begins with the following account of his writings:

> I would like to say, first of all, what was the goal of my work during the last twenty years. It was not to analyze the phenomenon of power, nor to elaborate the foundations of such an analysis.
>
> My objective, instead, has been to create a history of the different modes by which, in our culture, human beings are made subjects. My work has dealt with three modes of objectification which transform human beings into subjects (*Beyond*, 208).

The movies that we have been considering in this chapter all revolve around subjectivity in a context of the constituents of power: Shakespeare, Jenny, Slumdog, Nina, and Bridget all struggle to realize their subjectivity, and use sexuality as a means of discovering and expressing themselves. Foucault is not so much interested in the nature of power as in the way in which human beings learn to express themselves within the structures of power:

> The conclusion would be that the political, ethical, social, philosophical problem of our days is not to try to liberate the individual from the state, and from the state's institutions, but to liberate us both from the state and from the type of individualization that is linked to the state. We have to promote new forms of subjectivity through the refusal of this kind of individuality which has been imposed on us for several centuries (*Beyond*, 216).

Foucault explains that the struggles for new kinds of subjectivity are "not exactly for or against the individual but rather they are struggles against the 'government of individuation'" (*Beyond*, 212). Present-day governmental powers of individuation are the equivalent of what in the past, according to Foucault, was the power of the church, the pastoral control of individuals. Since the eighteenth century, the pastoral power of the church has been replaced by the secular reins of government, which is empowered in most democracies by the controls, or what Foucault calls the blocking of discipline, that is, the constraints or rules: "These blocks, in which the putting into operation of technical capacities, the game of communications and relationships of power are adjusted to one another according to considered formulae constitute what one might call, enlarging a little the sense of the word, disciplines" (*Beyond*, 219).

How power operates upon us, Foucault continues, is:

> [...] less a confrontation between two adversaries or the linking of one to the other than a question of government. This word must be allowed the very broad meaning it had in the sixteenth century. "Government" did not refer only to political structures or to the management of states; rather it designated the way in which the conduct of individuals or groups might be directed, the government of children, of souls, of communities, of families, of the sick. It did not only cover the legitimately constituted forms of political or economic subject action, but also modes of action, more or less considered and calculated, which are destined to act upon the possibilities of action of other people. To govern, in this sense, is to structure the possible field of action of others (*Beyond*, 221).

The power Foucault has in mind is that exercised in an "open" society over citizens who are "free." The individual negotiates this kind of power by way of strategic action.

> The word "strategy" is currently employed in three ways. First, to designate the means employed to obtain a certain end; it is a question of rationality functioning to arrive at an objective. Second, to designate the manner in which a partner in a certain game acts with regard to what he thinks should be the action of others and what he considers the others think to be his own; it is the way in which one seeks to have the advantage over others. Third, to designate the procedures used in this situation of confrontation to deprive the opponent of his means of combat and to reduce him to giving up the struggle; it is a question therefore of the means destined to obtain the victory (*Beyond*, 224–5).

Brute power is seldom our daily concern. Rather our life is filled with the quotidian intermingling of our individual strategies within the constraints of the power of discipline: what the literary critic struggles with in every sentence of the literature and of his or her commentary; what I am struggling with in this sentence. Strategy is learned, Foucault suggests, by courtship or the games of sexuality And he concludes that "what makes the domination of a group, a caste, or a class, together with the resistance and revolt which that domination comes up against, a central phenomenon in the history of societies is that they manifest in a massive and universal form, at the level of the whole social body, the locking together of power relations with relations of strategy and the results proceeding from their interaction" (*Beyond*, 226).

The implications for the literary critic are not different in kind from those in other intellectual disciplines or from those of the man in the street who is subject to the powers of government. All need to understand the nature of the constraints of the various disciplines imposed upon them or that they choose to impose upon themselves for the purpose of altering the "government of individuation." We are all then obliged to deconstruct power to arrive at "power-knowledge," not only in our various professions or disciplines, but as individuals seeking basic forms of self-expression. Whether a playwright, slumdog, dancer, student, or diarist, we must understand "power-knowledge" and negotiate the constraints of disciplines if we are to enjoy our limited freedoms:

> The relationship proper to power would not therefore be sought on the side of violence or of struggle [...] but rather in the area of the singular mode of action, neither warlike nor juridical, which is government (*Beyond*, 221).

Foucault's modification of author to "author-function" and of knowledge to "power-knowledge" leads to the question of the next chapter: within the discourse of "power-knowledge," how does the "author-function" communicate to the audience?

CHAPTER THREE

Reception theory: Wolfgang Iser

Summary: *After some background information on the forebears of reception theory, I begin with the hermeneutic circle that helps to decode "The Da Vinci Code." Two elements in this process, otherness and imagination, are clarified in the context of "Amélie," the story of a young woman who uses her imagination to help others. The interpretive or hermeneutic process involves, for Iser, filling in blanks or gaps, the subject of "Run Lola Run." Interpretation is seen as subject to historical change, which leads to Iser's use of the concept of "horizons of expectation," illustrated by "A Single Man," a film about the change during the past 50 years in our attitudes to male homosexuality. Here we confront intentionality and ethics because interpretation seeks ultimate artistic goals that are marked by distinct ethical questions. For instance, at the end of "The Godfather: Part III" we ask why we should be interested in criminals, what ethical goal is served by this mafia epic. This discussion raises the question of the cultural function of new perspectives, in "Vicky Cristina Barcelona" and "The King's Speech."*

At this point the reader may feel that my interpretation of the movies goes too far, making more of them than is warranted, particularly considering that they are all commercial ventures designed primarily for maximum box office profit. At about this stage of the undergraduate class in which this technique developed, the students began to ask questions about my approach in general, and in particular with regard to the movies that they considered of no artistic value because commercially successful. I pointed out that Shakespeare, having made his fortune on the London stage, went home to Stratford, bought a coat of arms, and had no interest in preserving his plays. And Samuel Johnson said that "no one but a blockhead ever wrote except for money." In short, most of our greatest literary and artistic treasures are the result of commercial ventures. Like any other profession, art may be corrupted by money and success but not necessarily. As for interpretation, the students suggested that this was all a matter of individual response; in other words, completely subjective.

The entire issue of interpretation central to reception theory is the topic of this chapter. Wolfgang Iser deconstructs the traditional notion that the only alternative to the accepted position opens the door to complete subjectivity. Iser points to a middle ground between these two extremes, presenting a method for excluding some but not eliminating all innovative interpretations. Reception theory is important because it provides a means of mediating between ultimate differences, not only for literary interpreters but also for people in general. No single view can be valid for everyone or withstand the test of time. Rather, for the reception theorist, responding to art involves a conversation between the work of art and the responder, in which each listens to and is heard by the other. And clearly, genuine conversation across real differences, particularly ideological ones, is of crucial concern to all of us.

Reception theory evolves from the position of a group of early twentieth-century German scholars who believed that the Bible needed to be interpreted rather than taken in literal terms, and also from the school of philosophy known as phenomenology. The key notion that developed from the combination was the hermeneutic circle, the circle of interpretation, the belief that in the arts and other distinctly human endeavors the results of interpretive analyses are inextricably bound up with the questions posed. Our individual approach to art limits what we take away from it: questions and answers together form the hermeneutic circle. Interpretations change in history and people vary in their responses from one another and from themselves, that is, they change their own approach. But an understanding of the interpretive process involves analysis of the relationship between beginnings and endings, questions and answers.

Iser insists that reception theory responds to a more recent problem:

[Reception theory] was engendered by the dilemma in which the study of literature found itself in the late 1950s and 1960s: namely, the conflict of interpretation. The cultural heritage no longer served as an unquestioned means of promoting what used to be called *Bildung* [education]; it became a problem because there were no longer uniform guidelines for such education, as had been the case in the past. Until the advent of modern art it was taken for granted that texts had a content, which was considered as a carrier of meaning. Interpretation had to uncover the text's meaning, which legitimized the whole process because meanings were considered to represent values that could be employed for the purpose of education [...] Eventually, this situation created an awareness of the fact that the presuppositions governing interpretation were to a large extent responsible for what the text was supposed to mean. Therefore the claim to have found *the* meaning implied justification of one's own assumptions and presuppositions, and this triggered what has since become known as the conflict of interpretation (*How to do*, 58).

The attempt to resolve the conflict of interpretation assumes the need for interpretation. But at this point, students often asked why do we need to interpret at all, why not simply appreciate and enjoy, particularly since films seem to be made for that purpose. To respond to this question and to introduce reception theory, I turn to another very famous and commercially successful film, "The Da Vinci Code" (2006), directed by Ron Howard, starring Tom Hanks, Audrey Tautou, and Ian McKellen. Although Iser applies his theory to literary fiction, I use film to explain certain of his ideas because most films, other than documentaries, are fictional, tell stories, or imply some narrative progression.

Hermeneutic interpretation: "The Da Vinci Code"

This film begins and ends in the Louvre and focuses upon the miniature double "V" at the heart of the Pei pyramid. To understand the hermeneutic circle of "The Da Vinci Code," consider the conversation between Professor Langdon (Tom Hanks) and Sir Leigh Teabing (Ian McKellen) about whether Jesus Christ is a man-god or was married and had a child. Two factions of the Catholic Church take opposing positions on this issue. The Priory of Sion is devoted to protecting the descendant of the marriage of Mary Magdalene and Jesus Christ, while Opus Dei insists that Christ never married and sets about preventing any evidence to the contrary from surfacing.

This seemingly dry and intellectual theological controversy has terrible human consequences: the film begins with the murder of Jacques Saunière, a member of the Priory of Sion, by Silas, a monk who is a loyal follower of Opus Dei. Robert Langdon, an American academic who has come to Paris to give a lecture on ancient symbols, is believed by the French police inspector to be the murderer of Saunière. Sophie Neveu, the niece of Saunière, helps Langdon escape from the police so that together they can find out who is really responsible for the murder. But "The Da Vinci Code" is to be distinguished from a typical murder mystery in that the resolution involves not merely identifying and finding the killer but also breaking the code left by Saunière. That code involves documentation and evidence of Christ as a man, not a man-god, who fathered a child with Mary Magdalene. The murder is a means of capturing our interest and drawing us into the pursuit of the Da Vinci code, that is, into interpreting symbols and following their directions. Only by solving this problem of the code can Professor Langdon find the real murderer and understand why he has been set up as the main suspect.

The audience is as puzzled as Sophie and Robert; for us, following the plot line of the film, understanding it at the most basic level, also involves unraveling the Da Vinci code. In fact, Jacques Saunière leaves clues at his death that exemplify reception theory: his last act before dying is to provide Sophie and Robert with symbols and signs incomprehensible to others but evoking a response in them that, he hopes, will lead to the discovery of his assassin and to the evidence and documents of The Priory of Sion. In response to students who believe interpretation is not necessary for pleasure and appreciation, this film requires the audience, if only for purposes of enjoyment, to engage in the process of unraveling the code, an act of interpretation.

The process by which Sophie and Robert unravel the mystery and save themselves is also the means by which we understand the film. This procedure involves many of the elements of reception theory. First, Saunière must provide sufficient clues for Robert and Sophie to solve the code and yet not enough information for anyone else, particularly his assassins, to beat them to it. So he deliberately provides what Iser calls "gaps" or "blanks," ones that he hopes only Robert and Sophie will be able fill in correctly. Iser describes this procedure in the context of reading a text, but it applies equally to responding to a film:

> As no story can ever be told in its entirety, the text itself is punctuated by blanks and gaps that have to be negotiated in the act of reading. Whenever the reader bridges a gap, communication begins. The gaps or structured blanks [...] function as a kind of pivot on which the whole text–reader relationship revolves, because they stimulate the process of ideation to be performed by the reader on terms set by the text [*How to do*, 64].

For instance, when Robert is first shown the dead body of Saunière, he realizes that the police inspector is wrong in believing that the marks on the corpse are symbols of devil-worship. On the contrary, Robert recognizes that the marks on the body are designed to lead him to other clues in the Louvre, and thus begins the communication between the dead man and the professor. Moreover, Saunière has been clever enough to lead Robert and mislead the police inspector who, we later learn, is a member of the opposition group, Opus Dei, responsible for the assassination.

Another element of reception theory pertaining to this film is the relation between the means and ends of the hermeneutic circle. In fact, the movie is a series of concentric circles. The innermost circle concerns the police inspector who is led to believe by the bishop, a high-ranking member of Opus Dei, that Robert is the murderer. In the end the inspector realizes he has been duped. The means by which hermeneutic circles are shown to be erroneous are called by Iser "negation":

> There is, however, another place in the textual system where text and reader converge, and that is marked by various types of negation. Blanks and negations both control the process of meaning assembly in different ways. The blanks leave open the connections between textual perspectives. [...] The various types of negation invoke familiar and determinate elements of knowledge only to cancel them out. What is cancelled, however, remains in view, and thus brings about modifications in the reader's attitudes to what is familiar or determinate [*How to do*, 64–5].

The police inspector's assertion that the symbol on the dead body is one of devil worship is "cancelled" out by Robert, but what remains is the fact that Saunière deliberately used a sign that would appear to most as that of the devil but to Robert as a clue toward resolving the Da Vinci code.

The next circle involves Sir Leigh Teabing, the rich British historian. Robert and Sophie turn to him because he is an expert in the Holy Grail legend that he believes refers not to the traditional Arthurian vessel but to Mary Magdalene as the vessel of the child of Christ. But Teabing turns out to be the mastermind behind the murder of Saunière. Thus, this second circle, like the first, involves deception, forcing Sophie and Robert to begin again, to form a new interpretive circle. And finally, the last and largest circle, encompassing the other two, is the "rose line" that Robert finally sees as the bloodline, the realization that Sophie Neveu is the last surviving ancestor of Christ. This element of her ancestry has been kept secret to protect her from Opus Dei. Notice that the hermeneutic circle does not always end in resolution; as we have seen, it may be "cancelled" or "negated," suggesting that an alternative approach is likely to be more fruitful. The force that drives us to search for another more appropriate hermeneutic circle is the interpretive quest, one that is all-encompassing, connecting all of the blanks toward a coherent end or goal: "the reader's wandering viewpoint [...] travels between all these segments, its constant switching during the time flow [...] intertwines them [...] [thus] bringing forth a network" [*How to do*, 65].

The final circle of "The Da Vinci Code," however, is different from those within it. For Sophie is diffident and skeptical about her role as the daughter of the Savior. She points out to Robert that she cannot walk on water, and Robert suggests to her that the literal truth is less important than what she believes. So while the smaller circles led to false literal answers, Robert as the murderer, Leigh as the disinterested scholar, the final larger circle is the genuine hermeneutic, one based upon belief and documents, not, as in the other two circles, the deceptive appearance of empirical evidence. And the double "v" at the beginning and end of this circle represents the commingling of male and female, the belief that God cannot be characterized by or limited to any single gender. Understandably, "The Da Vinci Code," although popular and successful in box office terms, is highly controversial, some seeing it as a harmless fiction and others as a means to undermine "the truth." And reception theory suggests that harmless fiction and "the truth" are two distinct but not concentric hermeneutic circles, each leading to different interpretive consequences. "The Da Vinci Code" demonstrates that for reception theory interpretation is a teleological act, that is, it involves ultimate ends related to beginnings, and that hermeneutic circles change in history and vary with personal beliefs.

Perhaps the most vivid example of how negation operates within the hermeneutic circle in the film involves the clue, "Pope Alexander." Like Robert and Sophie, we assume that the reference is to a Pope called Alexander and seek out the burial place of this Pope. That expectation is thwarted, another indication that hermeneutic circles may lead to impasses requiring us to begin again from a new point of departure. Robert eventually realizes that the reference is to Alexander Pope, the British poet who the movie erroneously places at the funeral of Sir Isaac Newton at Westminster Abbey. Changed initial assumptions or first questions lead to different conclusions, not to a church in Rome but an abbey in London. Again, the negative or cancelled remains in that Pope Alexander is designed to mislead the enemy. And the answer to the students' questions about the need for interpretation is that it may not always save your life, as it does for Sophie and Robert, but it will enrich your life: "The Da Vinci Code" can be enjoyed as a "who done it" with esoteric references and lovely European setting, or as a film about the nature of an alternative to the traditional view of Christ as a man-god.

Here the relationship between reception theory and deconstruction becomes overt, since this Iserian reading of "The Da Vinci Code" concludes by exposing the traditional position on Christ as an originary myth. Iser explains in literary terms what I believe also applies to film: "Literature endeavors to counter the problem produced by systems through focusing on their deficiencies, thus enabling us to construct whatever was concealed or ignored by the dominant systems of the day At the same time the text must implicitly contain the basic framework of the systems concerned, as this is what causes the problems that literature reacts to" [How to do, 63].

Otherness and imagination: "Amélie"

Another commercially successful movie but one that focuses upon a protagonist who opts out of the system in a comic mode, "Amélie" (2001) is directed by Jean-Pierre Jeunet and stars Audrey Tautou. This film is about a young girl, raised by two eccentric parents, who as a result of her upbringing becomes herself very introverted and somewhat eccentric. The first section focuses on the individual differences and idiosyncrasies of taste that distinguish people from one another. Amélie likes to eat raspberries on her fingers; her mother adores cleaning her handbag and cannot abide grocers who touch her hands; her father loves to clean his tool-box and is uncomfortable when people stare at his sandals. These personality differences separate us as individuals and are related to our different responses to art. But the problem is that if these personal distinctions are permitted to become determinants in interpretation, the result is total subjectivity. For reception theory the question is how we accept individual responses and yet arrive at some interpretive consensus. In the terms of the film, the question is how Amélie will come out of her shell and yet maintain her special charm, her winning individuality.

The process by which Amélie moves out of herself and toward the outside world begins when she discovers a box of childhood treasures hidden behind the molding in her apartment. She immediately realizes that the "worthless" contents of this box mean a great deal to someone and sets out to discover who it is. But, in keeping with her introverted personality, she manages to return the property to its owner without appearing herself and without the owner knowing who is responsible for returning the box. However, in being at one remove from the moment of repossession she is able to observe how much happiness the retrieval has given to the owner who savors the souvenirs of his childhood. Amélie now finds that she can give pleasure by exploiting her sensitivity to the deep inner needs of others. She arranges for one of the habitués of the café where she works to have a relationship with the woman who is a fellow worker. She helps the young man at the local grocery who is bullied by his boss. Recognizing that the boss's sense of power derives from his certainty of his routine, she undermines his self-assurance. But perhaps her greatest accomplishment concerns her father. Living alone, mourning the loss of his wife, Raymond almost never leaves home, devoting himself instead to building a garden memorial to his late wife. Among the objects in this reliquary is his prize gnome. Amélie has the ingenious idea of stealing the gnome, then asking her friend, an airline stewardess, to send her father picture postcards of the gnome photographed in various exotic destinations. At first, her father is puzzled and troubled, but eventually he is intrigued, traveling to the various places on the postcards. Thus Amélie brings her father out of himself and into the world. In each of these instances, Amélie has established rapport with individuals by acts of empathy. Outwardly, she remains an introvert but inwardly she has become directed toward others. She has become a reception theorist, able to anticipate how others will respond in ways quite different from her own. At this point, "Amélie" has shown that individual responses need not necessarily lead to ultimate differences but can be a means of communication, a bridge to understanding otherness. But Amélie remains alone, and here the Glassman is crucial. He is the brittle-boned artist in her apartment building who can never venture outside. His physical dilemma is a mirror of Amélie's psychological one. He first comes into the story by helping Amélie find the owner of the box. Then he invites Amélie into his apartment and shows her his paintings, all copies of Renoir's "Luncheon of the Boating Party." But one figure is causing him great difficulty because he cannot reproduce her expression. Looking at the original, Amélie suggests that the woman is probably preoccupied with her own thoughts, in a world not the same as that of the others in the picture, an imaginary realm.

Imagination is an important element of Iser's theory. "The imaginary has long been considered as a tangible manifestation of perfection, and it was assumed that art only allowed man's participation in it" [Future, 220]. But Iser insists that imagination must be understood in relation to reality. For instance, the Glassman realizes that in analyzing the woman in the painting Amélie is unconsciously describing herself. By this means the Glassman discovers the deeply sensitive imagination of Amélie, which we see throughout the film. Amélie's life is full of imaginary moments when she muses about how many people are having an orgasm or how her various co-workers could fall in love with one another. In fact her life is inhabited by the imagination, her best friend.

Iser explains that the imagination has an important function in our everyday perceptions:

> Whether the imaginary potential is viewed as perfection, otherness, the organizing faculty of cognition, unconscious fantasy, or desire, every one of these ontologically oriented definitions shows that it can only be grasped by way of its function and so in relation to contexts, which may be a counter-image to existing realities, a world shaken by inspiration, an organized interplay of cognitive faculties, an explanatory schema for the interpenetration of the conscious and unconscious, or a deprivation that cries out for expression [Future, 221].

Through his telescope, the Glassman sees Amélie using her imagination in all of these ways, most particularly the last, "a deprivation that cries out for expression." And he devises a clever means of "expression," rather like Amélie's own ploys, by suggesting that Amélie must not only attend to the needs of others but also to her own. He communicates this message to Amélie by way of a video in which he explains that if Amélie does not go out in quest of love and companionship she will end up like himself, a recluse never venturing out of his apartment. The Glassman resorts to a video because Amélie has sent him one, and he thus comes to realize, as we do watching the film, that Amélie is reticent about confronting people directly, resorting instead to visual media as a surrogate for conversation. In that sense, Amélie is a child of post-modern discourse, in particular, visual media, and we should not be surprised to find that her first successful relationship with a man is accomplished by way of pictures.

In fact, the final stage in Amélie's emergence into the world is accomplished by way of a photo album. The owner dropped the album in haste and Amélie tracked him down by way of a cat and mouse game that enabled each to see the other without being seen. In this way, each could decide if they were attracted to and interested in the other without making any prior commitment. Here we see another element of Iser's reception theory: the function of games or play.

Play also structures the interpenetration of the fictional and the imaginary, without determining the relationship, which unfolds itself in a veritable welter of games. It simultaneously allows us to reverse the games we play, and thus erase the definite imprint made on the relationship in order to manifest the imaginary differently. As play proceeds, any control exercised by thinking, the interplay between the conscious and the imaginary highlights the fact that neither exists independently of the other. There are no formal boundaries to this interplay, even though every particular work plays the game in its own way. Indeed, the game itself becomes a means of making present that which defies definition, while those elements of the imaginary that are to be observed through the literary work can only be mirrored forth by way of the game [*Future*, 224].

Of course, Amélie plays games with Nino because she is intrigued by the photo album. Here we see another instance of the interplay between the imagination and reality. Nino pieces together fragments of discarded passport photos much as Amélie attempts to give coherence to the fragmented emotional lives of her friends and acquaintances. And these others who fascinate her by way of their otherness present themselves to her like the torn photos in Nino's album, psychological snapshots of those who throw away the scraps of themselves, having lost hope in making their mark in the world or achieving full individuality.

The result of the games played by Amélie and Nino, a result that, as Iser might have put it, may not have been foreseen, is that they fall in love, discovering that they have similar interests, enjoy playing similar games.

Iser explains that one of the functions of reception theory is that it produces "self-enlightenment of the human being—not to be brought about by the erstwhile encyclopedic accumulation of knowledge considered to be a prerequisite for education, but by elucidating our unconscious guidelines, thereby triggering a chronic process of reflection which no longer seeks its fulfillment in some kind of ideal. Rather, this process will enable us to see through the attitudes offered to us, if not imposed upon us by our everyday world" [*Future*, 226].

Amélie has reconciled herself to the self-image of one who facilitates the love of others and now is surprised to find her own love reciprocated because Nino has a similar self-image. But the conclusion of the film makes this relationship emblematic of something larger, what Iser calls literary anthropology, or, by extension, what I would call artistic anthropology. We are led to see how the life of Amélie is related to the culture of Montmartre, the section of Paris so vividly presented throughout the film. In this regard, it is interesting that Jeunet, the writer and director of the film, lives in Montmartre across the street from the coffee shop, "The Two Windmills," that as a result of the film has become a tourist attraction, as has Collignon's market around the corner.

The film finally grounds itself in cultural reality with the explanation of the person who appears repeatedly in the photo album, whom Amélie thinks must be its creator. In the end we learn that he is the repairman of the photo machines and that the many photos of him are merely products of his tests of the machines. We joined with Amélie in imagining all sorts of complex psychological explanations for this man's seeming obsession with his own image, and share her surprise when a more mundane solution presents itself. Iser accounts for this procedure as follows:

> What at first seemed to be an affirmation of our assumptions leads to our own rejection of them, thus tending to prepare us for a re-orientation. And it is only when we have outstripped our preconceptions and left the shelter of the familiar that we are in a position to gather new experiences [...] [we are involved] in the formation of illusion and the simultaneous formation of the means whereby the illusion is punctured [*NLH*, 141].

The scraps of the many pictures of this man could be seen as a symbol of the fragmented existence of unfortunate people who, like Amélie, are for one reason or another isolated and self-absorbed. Now that we know that the photo repairman is a normal member of the community, we are led to understand that modern urban existence is itself fragmented, an experience that most inhabitants feel in one way or another, an awareness that brings together Amélie and Nino. Our response to the emergence of the relationship of Amélie and Nino and the context in which it occurs leads us to understand something about the culture of Montmartre, of urban culture, or our own culture: "[art] intervenes in its real environment and establishes its uniqueness not least by highlighting its otherness in relation to the situations that have conditioned it. In this manner it adumbrates new regions which it inscribes into the already chartered topography of culture. For if what is, is not everything, what is must be changeable" [*Future*, 227]. What changes for Amélie is that instead of finding love for others she finds it for herself. And we discover that fragmentation of self and of daily life is not exclusive to Amélie but a part of urban life, our culture.

Gaps or blanks and imagination: "Run Lola Run"

I turn now to how the reader's imagination functions in the interpretive process to fill in the "gaps" or "blanks." Again, Iser formulates blanks in terms of reading literature, but in the largest sense most human problems are subject to a process analogous to reading: successful conversation, two people using their imagination to understand one another, involves a similar process:

> Blanks indicate that the different segments and patterns of the text are to be connected even though the text itself does not say so. They are the unseen joints of the text, as they mark off patterns and textual perspectives from one another, and simultaneously prompt acts of ideation on the reader's part. Consequently, when the patterns and perspectives have been linked together, the blanks "disappear" (*How to do*, 65).

The notion of gaps, or blanks, is illustrated by a movie entitled "Run Lola Run." Written and directed by Tom Tykver, the film first appeared in 1998, starring Franka Potente as Lola and Moritz Bleibtreu as Manni. This movie is particularly pertinent to reception theory because it is divided up into three parts, each of which is a different version of essentially the same story. The differences between the three versions have to do with how the blanks or gaps are filled in. And blanks or gaps are important because they are not merely different means to the same end but also to different ends, to how the story (stories) concludes. All three versions share the same problem, the reason Lola runs is that her boyfriend Manni needs to raise 100,000 Deutschmarks or face terrible punishment, perhaps even death. Another common thread in all versions is that, once Lola receives the call for help from Manni, she runs out of an apartment where her mother is on the phone discussing the daily horoscope and descends the stairway to be confronted by a boy and his dog. The spiral staircase scene is reminiscent of a famous scene in Hitchcock's "Vertigo," an archetypal symbol of the beginning of a journey with a mysterious end.

Because Lola has only 20 minutes to get the money, the amount of time lost in getting around the boy and his dog is crucial to the outcome. In the first version, the dog barks at Lola, frightening her into running faster. In the second version the dog trips her up, delaying her, and in the third version Lola jumps over the dog, gaining a few seconds on the first two versions. At first viewing, it might appear that this initial difference in the time taken descending the staircase is sufficient to account for the three different outcomes. But there are also psychological factors involving response and reception. For instance, in version one, Lola runs in front of a car, causing an accident, and therefore arrives at the bank at the moment when it becomes clear from her father's conversation that he is having an affair with a colleague. Now that Lola knows about his affair, when she asks her father for money he not only refuses but also tells her that she is not his daughter. Lola's response is to run to the aid of Manni, only to find him in the midst of the holdup that results in her death. We may infer that her disappointment or despair have contributed to her death.

By the second version we begin to understand what the gaps are because they are filled in a different way. On this occasion, Lola, arriving a bit later, learns that her father's mistress, a member of the board of directors of the bank, is pregnant by another man. Angry now not just at her father but also at his mistress, Lola decides to rob the bank, taking the money to Manni. Unfortunately, he is run over by an ambulance before she can get to him. As a result of robbing the bank she arrives too late to rescue Manni. We may infer that Lola's disgust at the bank's managers has contributed to her being too late to help Manni.

The third version fills in the blanks in still another way. Lola jumps over the dog, thereby avoiding the car accident that happened in the two earlier versions. One of these cars, we now learn, is meant to pick up Lola's father for a luncheon appointment. When Lola gets to the bank her father is gone. She therefore goes to a casino, winning more than enough money to cover Manni's debt. Meanwhile, finding the homeless man who has taken his money, Manni trades his gun for the money. We are again left to decide or fill in the blanks by way of interpretation: what drove Lola to risk all of her winnings at the casino and what led Manni to believe that the homeless man still had his money. And the psychological element is emphasized by the scenes between the three versions of Lola and Manni in bed together asking one another questions about love and death, establishing that the basic drive for both is their desire to save one another, a point reinforced at the end of the film when they walk away delighted simply to be safe and with one another, Manni unaware that Lola has won possibly the equivalent of the lottery.

This movie makes clear that gaps or blanks in human situations are complex because they involve not just responses but responses to responses, like that between Lola and her father or between Lola and Manni. In life, the result of human interaction often changes the end results in spite of limitations of space and time. In reception theory, the limitations of space and time are represented by a work of art, most notably a story, and our response to art changes not the actual end but our interpretation of the end. Reception theory assumes the importance of interpretation. One may view "Run Lola Run" as no more than three versions of how the contingencies of space and time affect our lives. But that would fail to account for the fact that Manni and Lola are marginals in a bourgeois society comprised of people like Lola's mother, complacently encapsulated in her own world, and her father, successful in commercial terms but deeply unhappy with his wife and "weird" daughter. Furthermore, we are left with no explanation of why Manni gives the gun to the homeless man who has taken his money. An interpreter of the film might surmise that Manni feels an affinity with the beggar, another marginal in a society dominated by bourgeois prosperity and middle-class comfort. Reception theory encourages us to draw inferences about what makes Lola run, namely, that love for Manni distinguishes her from her family, a factor that can lead to tragic or comic consequences.

The manner in which interpretation is a key factor in our lives, not just in our approach to art, is illustrated in the movie by the different inset scenarios for the people Lola sees on her run. For instance, in each version Lola passes quickly by a woman pushing a baby stroller. The film gives us a parenthesized imaginary sequence of what happens to her in the future, each version related to how she responds to Lola. In version one, she kidnaps a baby after social services has taken away her child. In version two, she wins the lottery, and in version three, she has a religious conversion. Each inset scenario is related to Lola's response to the woman's different responses. Inferences we draw from human interaction are key to artistic interpretation and are a part of our daily conversations with others.

These inset scenarios make emphatic the role of the imagination in the act of interpretation. For Iser, interpretation is a quest for "intentionality," a term derived from phenomenology that means not so much the intention of the artist but the ultimate goal of the work of art. This distinction becomes less obscure when applied to everyday life: in conversation we often experience someone announcing an intention quite different from what his or her words communicate—as when people say "sorry" but mean "please move out of my way." Intentionality, what someone is really getting at, is often different from that expressed by the speaker's assertion of intention. The process of seeking intentionality requires, for Iser, the imagination.

The relationship between the imagination and interpretation of the story or "fiction" involves what Iser calls "play." In this regard, it is important to recall that after a brief introduction, "Run Lola Run" begins with a referee throwing a soccer ball into the air, announcing, "Let play begin." Keeping in mind that the inset scenarios seem to be imaginings of Lola concerning people she sees on her run, the following description is apt:

> [...] the imaginary has no intentionality of its own but has intentions imposed on it by the demands of its activator. And precisely because it is without intentionality, it appears to be open to all intentions that will always be tied to what they trigger, so that something will "happen" to the activator. Thus the imaginary can never be identical to its intention-led mobilization [...] Instead the imagination exposes itself in interplay with its different activators. This interplay is identical neither to the intentions nor to the imaginary gestalt that it brings about, although this gestalt could not come into being without the intention-led mobilization of the imaginary [*The Fictive*, 223].

Consider again the woman with the pram. Lola is clearly the activator of these imaginary digressions; she alone has the intentionality of the story, to bring Manni the money on time. From Lola's point of view, the woman is merely an obstruction, although there is no indication that such is the woman's "intention." Each different scenario of this woman is determined by Lola's imaginative interpretation of the woman's view of her. Imagination thus serves as the tool of interpretation, which involves a conception of an end-goal, from the woman becoming a criminal to her experiencing a religious conversion. We are thus encouraged to use our imagination to interpret "Run Lola Run," to see the intentionality of the film as beyond that of getting the money to Manni on time.

Since for Iser imagination is a key element of the interpretive process, it is not seen as a faculty of mind apart from reality that serves the purposes of fantasy. Rather it intermingles with the reality or the seemingly real of a story to help us discover an artistic goal. In the film, we have a vivid example of this notion. In the first two versions, a man tries to sell Lola his bike; he is marginal, a subject of Lola's imagination. In the final version, however, the homeless man buys the bike and it now becomes a part of the main story, suggesting how the marginal and imaginative can enter into reality or the seeming reality of fiction, because the bike clearly serves a purpose, in this case, a means of transport for the homeless man. Iser explains as follows: "Since the transitory nature of play in the ordinary world is geared to goals that may be achieved a philosophy of play needs to postulate purposes" [*The Fictive*, 224]. And discovering purpose involves selectivity, decisions about what is more or less important in advancing a narrative to its conclusion. Often, as in "Run Lola Run," the selection involves multiple texts, the different runs and the various inset scenarios, or what Iser calls clusters of texts or "intertextuality": "The clustering adds to the complexity of play space, for the allusions and quotations take on new dimensions in relation to both their old and their new contexts.

Since both old and new remain potentially present, there is a coexistence of different discourses that reveal their respective contexts as a play of alternating fade-ins and fade-outs" [*The Fictive*, 227]. In the end, when Lola and Manni walk down the street happily, the previous two runs are not erased. Rather, we infer that the same forces and factors that resulted in the deaths of Lola and Manni in the earlier versions have played a part in the last version. Whether they live or die has little to do with their individual goals, their intentionality; they are in fact pawns in a matrix, controlled by larger forces beyond their control. Perhaps the "intentionality" of this film is that we hold tenaciously to interpretation as our only element of ultimate control, uncertain whether or not that is also our ultimate illusion, simultaneously running toward and away from it.

Nevertheless, the hermeneutic circle, the act of interpretation, is itself bound by the limitations of space and time, that is, by the responder's historical/cultural situation vis à vis that of the work of art. Here we encounter another major idea of reception theory, horizons of expectation. To explain this notion Iser makes use of the formulation of his colleague, Hans Robert Jauss.

> [Reception theory] tries to grasp prevailing attitudes that have shaped the understanding of a literary work in a given period of time [...] it seeks to reconstruct the "horizons of expectation" entertained by the reading public which, in determining what is considered artistic, revealed its own standards. In this respect reception functions as a divining rod for tracing the recipients' taste at a particular historical moment. [...] By delineating the historical conditionality of readers' reactions, an aesthetics of reception turns literature into a tool for reconstituting the past (*How to do*, 57).

Horizons of expectation: "A Single Man"

An excellent example of "horizons of expectation" is provided by the recent movie entitled "A Single Man" (2009), directed by Tom Ford and starring Colin Firth as George Falconer, a gay university professor. This movie takes place in Southern California in 1962, a historical reference that makes clear almost immediately why reception theorists use the plural "horizons" rather than the singular "horizon": the assumption is that interpretation involves an interplay between the horizons of the past and present, or between that of the responder and that implicit in the work of art. In this particular film, there is a clear relationship between the conventions of being a male homosexual in 2009, when the film first appeared, as opposed to 1962. The plot is very straightforward. George has recently lost his long-term partner in an automobile accident. But his mourning, however intense, is repressed for two reasons. First, the family of his long-term partner never acknowledged George as the partner of their son and refused to allow him to attend the funeral. Second, in the middle-class culture of California of the 1960s, it was not considered seemly for a gay man, particularly a professor, someone with regular access to young people, overtly to mourn the loss of his lover.

Yet the movie itself is an intense expression of grief to us, the audience, while a very delicate and restrained display of George's sadness to his contemporaries, except for his one close friend. We witness both forms of grief as a result of knowing something George tells no one, namely, that he, in despair, is preparing to commit suicide. In this sense the film is about the two contrasting "horizons of expectation" between now and then. On the one hand, George can only discreetly indicate his deep sadness to his closest friends, but, on the other hand, to us the depth of his mourning is palpable. In my view, Colin Firth deftly intermingles the two "horizons of expectation": his controlled, quiet sadness with his contemporaries simultaneously suggests to the present-day audience an inconsolable loss; and indeed he received a BAFTA award for his portrayal of George. As Iser's colleague, H. R. Jauss, suggested, the contrast of horizons is often of historical significance. Attitudes toward gay male couples have changed markedly since 1962.

In fact, the world of the gay man has changed. Tom Ford is himself gay and, like the character in the movie, has lived with a partner for many years. Moreover Ford, a well-known clothes designer, dresses George and indeed the entire movie with impeccable, unpretentious, expensive taste. As George in the movie controls his existence and restricts his emotional expression by being meticulous in dress and behavior, so Ford the director is, in a sense, ostentatiously understated in his *mise en scène*. Interestingly, some reviewers have objected to the overly controlled design of the sets and décor on the ground that it is rather like being in a designer's salon, but I wonder if Ford deliberately chose to call attention to the film as a "gay" production, suggesting perhaps that the present gay "scene" still requires discreet taste. In any event, the critics' objections are of historical significance, suggesting that gay directors have not yet achieved total acceptance in our society.

Nonetheless, the movie makes clear that major cultural changes have occurred. One of my favorite scenes involves George's evening with his female friend, a heterosexual divorcée, Charlie, played by Julianne Moore. Aware of George's love for his late partner, Charlie empathizes with his grief but then makes a pass at him, suggesting a conflicted attitude. As a homosexual George is a trusted friend and confidant, but as an attractive man she hopes he will recover "normalcy" and respond to her sexual advances. Similarly, the neighbor, a woman with a husband and two children, invites George to her cocktail party, yet her daughter tells George that her father describes him as "light in his loafers." The marginality of homosexuals in 1962 explains George's suicidal tendencies. Yet he dies of a heart attack shortly after deciding not to commit suicide.

We are left with a number of possible interpretations of this conclusion. Since the heart condition precedes his relationship with his late lover, perhaps the most deep-seated problem for him is not the loss of his partner but the alienation of the homosexual, resulting finally in a broken heart. Alternatively, George's heart attack could be brought on by his uneasy feeling about the young male student who is persistently pursuing and perhaps tempting him. Does George feel disloyal to his late partner, or is he afraid of losing his "respectability" by debauching a young man? Does he feel that the young man pursuing him has little understanding of his deep loyalty to his late partner? Still a third alternative might focus upon George's discovery that the young man has found the gun and taken it to prevent George's suicide. For a moment, and it is perhaps the only such moment in the film, George appears pleased and happy, stating that it is for him one of the rare glimpses of "clarity." Is the clarity about finding a new lover, someone who genuinely cares about him, or is he finally reconciled to his position as a quietly discreet misfit in a society desperately holding on to a male machismo worldview?

The conclusion is open to these many possibilities precisely so that many different kinds of responses can be accommodated. For all involve interplay between the horizons of expectation of 1962 and those now current concerning male homosexuality. As Jauss indicated, we are thereby made aware of the change in our attitude to this phenomenon, to its history. "A Single Man" tells us that we have come a long way since 1962 but still have a long way to go. Here we begin to see that the anthropological element of reception theory is more than merely descriptive of our culture; it arrives at an ethical imperative. Our feeling of sadness at the end of this film, not only for the untimely death of George but also for his entire life of repression, even rejection by the family of his lover, leads to a question. Even now, have we done enough to improve the life of homosexuals in our world?

Ethics and intentionality: "The Godfather: Part III"

While reception theory opens up interpretation to more than one possibility, it establishes clear limitations. As we have seen, Iser insists that the gaps and blanks must be provided by the text, limiting the range of possible readings. But also, reception theory is committed to the concept of the teleology of the text, namely, that artists usually make clear what is their ultimate goal, their intended conclusion. Iser makes this point in his critique of mimesis, the belief that art imitates nature. "Forms, it appears, are not so much constitutive conditions of Nature as images remembered by the artist, who projects these onto what is given in such a way that the beholder also sees Nature in a manner intended by the artist" [*The Fictive*, 285]. And the intention of the artist is usually to be found in the ethical ramifications of the conclusion of the work of art.

For instance, Francis Ford Coppola's "The Godfather: Part III" (1990) contains a climactic scene that prepares us for the conclusion, a kind of coda in which an elderly Michael Corleone in an armchair dies all alone. The opera "Cavalleria Rusticana" has been carefully chosen. And we have been prepared for its significance. Announcing proudly that his son Anthony will sing the lead in the opera, Michael is interrupted by his son, who corrects his father's pronunciation of the title. Uncharacteristically, the godfather accepts his son's correction, remarking that "I have been living in New York for too long." Coppola calls our attention to this opera because it is a fitting conclusion to his three-part epic about the Mafia.

We are shown the staging of this opera so that we can understand how it applies to the story of the Corleone family. Unlike most operas, "Cavalleria Rusticana" is exclusively about peasants and, most appropriately, Sicilian peasants. The action, we can gather from what we are shown in the film, concerns a rivalry between two families about love and concludes with the murder of the protagonist by one of the rival families. During the staging of the film we see in the audience action analogous to that of the opera in the form of thwarted love and murder. Michael has forbidden a relationship between Mary and Vincent, and the rival mafia gang tries to kill Michael and Anthony, eventually murdering Mary. Although the analogy between the final action of the film and the opera is by no means perfect or complete, Coppola signals the significance of the analogy when on the steps of the opera house after the murder the camera draws back from the carnage that includes the bodies of the assassins while the remainder of the cast form themselves into a symmetrical pattern around the victims, rather like the final moment in a tragic opera.

Reception theory suggests that in this manner Coppola is indicating that his entire three-part epic on the Mafia is a sort of opera for the audience. The point then becomes less about the Mafia itself and more about our interest in and response to tales of the Mafia, which can be taken, like opera itself, as at once fantastical and melodramatic and as an exaggerated version of reality. For Iser has already warned us that the imaginary and the real are never completely separated.

The technique employed here by Coppola is suggested by Iser's concept of "staging."

Staging in literature makes conceivable the extraordinary plasticity of human beings, who, precisely because they do not seem to have a determinable nature, can expand into an almost unlimited range of culture-bound patternings. [...] [Thus] literature becomes a panorama of what is possible because it is not hedged in either by the limitations or the considerations that determine the institutional organizations within which human life otherwise takes it course [*The Fictive*, 297].

We witness the staging for the Corleones of the origins of the Mafia. The purpose of such an exercise, it seems to me, is to lead us to ask why we are interested in the Mafia. Do we perhaps believe that the "legal" establishment operates in a similar way? Or do we maybe wish that the government could resort to Mafia methods—as some assume has happened at Guantanamo? In either case, reception theory changes the focal point of interpretation from the Mafia itself to our response to the Mafia. This sort of interpretive turn is particularly useful as many artists, particularly contemporary ones, stage events for the purpose of evoking and making us aware of our response to art rather than merely from an interest in the intrinsic nature of the artifact.

The ethical impact of this conclusion is unmistakable. Are we content to accept a "legal" society that in some respects resembles that of the Mafia? Are we willing to subject our children to dangers like that experienced by Mary Corleone? Or are we merely being complacent in assuming that such an analogy is far-fetched? In this way, reception theory points to the "plasticity of human beings" that permits us to put ourselves in the place of the Mafia and ask such ethical questions. The hermeneutic circle of interpretation is not merely circular, leading us back to ourselves, or self-consciousness, but, in the context of art, leads us to see ourselves and our culture from a new perspective.

The function of perspectives: "Vicky Cristina Barcelona"

An excellent example of two acceptable hermeneutic circles within the same situation is provided by "Vicky Cristina Barcelona" (2008), written and directed by Woody Allen, starring Scarlett Johansson, Rebecca Hall, Javier Bardem and Penelope Cruz. This movie is about two young American women who spend a summer vacation together in Barcelona. Although together for most of their time abroad and sharing an attraction to the same man, they end with very different views of the experience. One important reason for this difference is that, although long-time, close friends, they approach this summer holiday in different ways, from different beginnings. Engaged to be married to Doug, an American back at home, Vicky comes to Barcelona to study Catalan culture, the subject of her research project.

By contrast, her friend Cristina is unattached and therefore more open to the social and sexual scene. Shortly after their arrival, the two beautiful women are approached by Juan Antonio, a young Catalan painter, who invites them on a short jaunt to a nearby small town. Eventually each of the women has an intimate relationship with Juan Antonio, but the experience itself and the results are quite different

What is interesting about this movie from the point of view of reception theory is that, although both women share the same experience, living together for the summer and having sex with the same man, their lives take very different turns as a result of this holiday, that is, each woman interprets the experience in unique terms. Cristina becomes involved in a "*ménage à trois*" with Juan Antonio and his previous girlfriend, Maria Elena. Although happy with this arrangement for a while, she eventually comes to feel that it is not the right situation for her and leaves. Vicky marries Doug even though still attracted to Juan Antonio, but cannot then reconcile herself to divorcing Doug. Although the Barcelona summer experience is similar in many ways for the two women, they come away from it with very different views.

Cristina discovers that she provides the stability for the relationship of Maria Elena and Juan Antonio but feels too confined by their need of her. So, having initially been attracted by the social and sexual freedom of Catalan culture compared to that of the States, she now feels confined and constricted. Vicky, on the other hand, now married to an American, is still deeply moved and attracted to Catalan culture and to Juan Antonio but finds him too erratic and unreliable.

The title of the movie suggests that Woody Allen is interested in two perspectives on the same situation. The absence of "and" and "in" in the title indicates that the two women are the two eye-pieces of a microscope, looking at the same object but from a slightly different angle that combines for the audience to form a single image. We come away with a combination of the two women's perspectives: Catalan culture is in some respects freer and in others more confining than that of the United States. Cristina's and Vicky's decisions about which way of life they prefer is a function of individual values. Cristina's decision is negative: this way of life is not for her, so her search continues. Vicky is more conflicted: she longs for more romance but fears insecurity. Allen cleverly shows us two key aspects of Catalan culture by way of two hermeneutic circles: our hermeneutic circle, incorporating Vicky's and Cristina's, reveals that greater sexual freedom involves deeper personal and psychological entanglements, as in the relationship between Juan Antonio and Maria Elena. Different but related, Vicky and Cristina each have a viable grasp of an aspect of Catalan culture. Their hermeneutic circles have different beginnings and ends but touch upon one another like good friends walking hand in hand. By contrast, the audience's view, although including those of Vicky and Cristina, has the limitation of being that of onlookers, not participants. For we see moving pictures of Barcelona, but Vicki and Cristina go there and experience the culture. The circle of interpretation is never definitive; it is limited by beginnings, initial questions or quests and by the interpreter's knowledge and presuppositions. Reception theory insists that interpretation is a conversation between the work of art and she or he who seeks to understand it, and that the results will vary according to the limitations of the responder, the questions posed, and the historical era. For Iser this procedure whereby we see a "simulacrum" of ourselves—a projected image of what we could do or might be—"staged" is a key element of our humanity:

> Staging is the indefatigable attempt to confront ourselves with ourselves, which can be done only by playing ourselves. It allows us, by means of simulacra, to lure into shape the fleetingness of the possible and to monitor the continual unfolding of ourselves into possible otherness. We are shifted into ourselves, though this transposition does not make us able to coincide with what we are able to observe; it simply opens us up to the possibility of such transposing [*The Fictive*, 303].

Vicky and Cristina represent possibilities in Catalan culture open to us and for us that we may never wish or be able to pursue. Thus the final thrust of Iser's reception theory arrives at an ethical goal: by way of the empathy evoked by works of art we develop a tolerance for difference, whether of cultures, historical periods, or individuals. The contribution of reception theory is to open interpretation, human conversation at its best, to others and to historical change in ourselves and our culture.

Having now clarified how Iser deconstructs the interpretative process, opening it to individual differences, we turn in the next chapter to a modification of the concept of individuality, to Lacan's reassessment of the Freudian ego.

CHAPTER FOUR

Jacques Lacan and post-Freudianism

Summary: *Lacan believes the instinctive ego of Freud is a function of discourse. This deconstructed ego originates with the "mirror stage," when a child, aged between six months and 18 months, is held up by his or her parent to a mirror and given a name. This idea is extended to the adult world and explained by way of "The Queen." Three important consequences follow from this stage: 1) the unconscious as language, illustrated in "The Reader"; 2) transference as seen in "Frost/Nixon"; 3) imago as evidenced in "Lost in Translation." The final section shows how these three concepts relate to each other in the context of "L'Auberge espagnole" ("Pot Luck") and "The King's Speech."*

Lacan deconstructs Freud by asserting that for Freud the ego, comprised of instincts, reason, and morality—the id, ego, and super-ego—is in fact a function of language or discourse, a term used, as we have seen, for all forms of communication. This important innovation stems from "the mirror stage," an account of how a child at a very early period of its life, from six months to 18 months of age, develops a sense of self or personal identity. After an introduction to the "mirror stage" and "The Queen," I focus on three Lacanian notions that stem from the mirror stage: the unconscious as language in "The Reader," transference in "Frost/Nixon," and imago in "Lost in Translation." My conclusion involves an analysis of two films, "L'Auberge espagnole" ("Pot Luck") and "The King's Speech," that suggest a connection between these three ideas. But at the outset it is helpful to understand that all of the ideas stem from the mirror stage. The crucial point about the mirror stage is that the child is introduced not merely to his or her own image in the mirror but also, and more importantly, to his or her name and thereby to the language system of his or her culture. For Lacan, the fact that a child's first sense of selfhood or personal identity is by way of discourse is crucial, and all Lacan's other notions discussed in this chapter derive from that insight. Since language is the predominant element of discourse, we can expect that Lacan's psycholinguistic views will entail a reassessment of the relationship between literary characters and "real" people as well as affecting our concept of the self, that of the ego or personal identity.

Discourse and "the mirror stage": "The Queen"

Stephen Frears's film "The Queen" (2006), starring Helen Mirren as Queen Elizabeth II and Michael Sheen as Prime Minister Tony Blair, focuses upon discourse in the form of media events. The movie begins with the election victory procession of Tony Blair moving down The Mall towards Buckingham Palace, to be followed shortly—the film passes over the three-month interval between the two events—at the same location by the funeral procession of Princess Diana. These media events show how all-pervasive is the realm of discourse, involving words and pictures about the main figures but also and very importantly including within the event the public response to the event. The contrast between Blair and Diana is stark, made emphatic by the pictures of the people, applauding jubilantly and then, shortly thereafter, mourning, many in tears. The Prime Minister commands a staff that enables him to employ the media to gain a landslide victory. Diana, by contrast, dies in an accident caused at least in part by the paparazzi, and the first public comment heard (and seen) after her death is that of Diana's brother Earl Spencer blaming the media for hounding her to a premature death. We are thus introduced to the world of public discourse, a perilous realm where public figures must be adept at "spin" or risk being the victims of it. We would expect the Queen to be well used to this world, but she is confronted with a profound change of public behavior that she and her advisers are unable at first to understand. In short, public discourse presents the Queen with a mirror that she at first resists and then only gradually accepts.

Helen Mirren received an Academy Award for Best Actress for her performance as Queen Elizabeth II. I begin with this film because it demonstrates how the principle of the "mirror stage" pertains not only to infants but also to adults. A radical change of identity for the Queen of England occurs when she has been on the throne for nearly 50 years. Although the title of the film refers to the reigning monarch, the central action concerns how the Queen responds to the death of Princess Diana. Tony Blair's staff immediately turn their full attention to this event. However, the Queen at first insists that since Diana is divorced from Prince Charles her funeral should be considered a private, not a public matter. Blair and his staff recognize that the general public does not consider Diana to be completely separated from the royal family. Accordingly, Blair makes a major speech on Diana's death in which he refers to her, using the phrase of his trusted aide, Alistair Campbell, as "the people's princess," words that become the key element of discourse that reshapes the British monarchy.

In fact, the film is punctuated with discursive events that affect personal identity. Near the beginning of the film, Blair, newly elected as Prime Minister, is presented to the Queen, whose chief of protocol explains that one never turns one's back in "the presence," that is, when one is with the Queen. Blair is profoundly affected by "the presence," feeling at times the need to save her from herself and at others to defend her for her lengthy, selfless service to the country. Near the end of the movie, Cherie Blaire only half jestingly suggests that the Queen is for the Prime Minister a mother figure, preparation for the Queen's prophetic remarks to Blair, to be discussed later. Still another instance of a discourse event involves the Lord Chamberlain pronouncing the word precedent as "*pree*cedent," occasioning Blair to remark, "where do they find these people?" Alistair Campbell also finds the Lord Chamberlain's language and manner pompous and pretentious. Here the discourse serves to point up the class divide between the aristocratic court and the staff of a democratically elected politician. Another discourse event further emphasizing the distinction between classes occurs at the funeral when, after Diana's brother's speech, the audience inside and outside the church erupts into applause while the royal party refrains from any public display of emotion. Although all of these instances can serve to illustrate the mirror element of discourse, I focus on the "people's princess" because it involves a radical change of personal identity and becomes public discourse when the newspapers—a discursive medium made much of in the film—give it headline significance.

This phrase offends most members of the royal family. Indeed, the decision to make the funeral a public event with entertainment from such pop idols of the "people" as Elton John is regarded by the Queen, the Duke of Edinburgh, and the Queen Mother as vulgar and in poor taste. In their view, the funeral arrangements should be made by Diana's family, the Spencers. The royal family, therefore, do not alter their summer routine, remaining at their holiday retreat at Balmoral Castle in Scotland. In London and in many other parts of the world there is a huge outpouring of public grief for Diana. Masses of mourners gather at Buckingham Palace awaiting some word from the Queen. But for days she does not appear, and the tabloids begin to criticize her severely. Finally after a number of phone calls from Blair and the pleading of Prince Charles, the Queen decides to return to London.

Just before leaving Balmoral, she goes for a drive on her own through the woodlands of the estate, suddenly coming into sight of a majestic old stag that is being hunted. While the Duke stalks the animal, the Queen, struck by the beauty of the stag, drives it away from the hunters, but before her return to London she is told the stag has been killed by a commercial hunter on a neighboring estate. She then makes a visit to the magnificent dead animal suspended headless by its hind feet. Noticing that the stag has been wounded before dying, she expresses the hope that it did not suffer too much. Clearly, the Queen feels an affinity with the old deer hunted out of existence by, on the one hand, the old guard associated with the Duke of Edinburgh, and, on the other hand, the new moneyed class epitomized by the hunter. We are left with a sense that a part of her and of her monarchy is under threat and that change of a radical sort is in the wind.

Upon returning to London, the Queen wanders among the mourners at Buckingham Palace and is moved and surprised by the public display of emotion by her people, whom she had previously characterized as not prone to wearing their hearts on their sleeves. But to her credit, and here the great acting of Helen Mirren comes to the fore, the Queen adapts to this new concept of "the people's princess." Near the end of the film Tony Blair appears again before the Queen, now with a confident demeanor as the prime minister who has helped save the monarchy by insisting that the Queen adapt to the changing times. But the Queen, aloof and dignified, points out that what happened to her will also happen to Blair. And of course the audience knows by 2006, when the film was first released, that this is precisely what has happened, Blair having fallen out of favor and been replaced by Gordon Brown.

The conclusion of the movie demonstrates that while the Queen has adapted, and in some sense changed, there is also a fundamental sense in which she is still the Queen, able to maintain her independence from the political establishment. But for Lacanians the important issue is that the change or adaptation on the part of the Queen resulted from a cultural crisis signaled by discourse: "the people's princess," a phrase that was initially seen by the Queen and most members of the royal family as inappropriate, if not incomprehensible. One of the important principles of the mirror stage is a feeling of alienation and lack of control: the infant does not choose its name, and that chosen by its parents may feel as strange and mysterious to the child as the phrase "the people's princess" felt to the Queen. Alistair Campbell's choice of phrase to characterize Diana is not merely a lucky quip but a moment of insight that helps galvanize and articulate the mood of the historical moment. And the Queen comes to realize that she must accept this change in her subjects' attitude while herself feeling not at all comfortable with it. In this respect "The Queen" can be seen as an instance of the power of discourse to alter personal identity. Lacan describes this process as follows:

> The *mirror stage* is a drama whose internal thrust is precipitated
> from insufficiency to anticipation—and which manufactures for the
> subject, caught up in the lure of spatial identification, the succession
> of phantasms that extends from a fragmented body-image to a form of
> its totality that I shall call orthopaedic—and, lastly, to the assumption
> of the armour of an alienating identity, which will mark with its rigid
> structure the subject's entire mental development (*Ecrits*, 5).

Lacan is here describing the experience of a young child, but I believe that
a similar experience can be had by adults during what has been called an
"identity crisis." The Queen explains to Blair that she was deeply wounded
by the media's report that 25 percent of her subjects hated her. Moreover,
the process by which the Queen comes to understand how she is perceived
by the public is reminiscent of Lacan's description of the child's response to
the mirror stage:

> We have only to understand the mirror stage as *an identification*, in the
> full sense that analysis gives to that term; namely, the transformation
> that takes place in the subject when he assumes an image—whose
> predestination [...] is sufficiently indicated by the use, in analytic theory,
> of the ancient term *imago* (*Ecrits*, 2).

Like the imago, the larva leaving the cocoon, the Queen emerges from
her closed car, an unprecedented act, we are told, to mingle among the
mourners outside the gate of Buckingham Palace. She discovers a new
world of public expression of bereavement, a mood that encompasses her
even as she moves among the people in wonderment. She is visibly shaken
by a note placed on a bank of flowers, which reads: "You have blood on
your hands." And at that climactic moment, a child presents the Queen
with a bouquet that she assumes is for Diana, but the child says, "They are
for you." Lacan explains that the moment of discovery of identity, or, in
this instance, the Queen's first sense of a new identity, is at once comforting
and strange or alienating.

> The fact is that the total form of the body by which the subject antici-
> pates in a mirage the maturation of his power is given to him only as
> *Gestalt*, that is to say, in an exteriority in which this form is certainly
> more constituent than constituted [...] symbolizing the mental perma-
> nence of the I, at the same time as it prefigures its alienating destination
> (*Ecrits*, 3).

The Queen is gratified by the child's gesture but taken aback at the new
kind of role that is expected of her. She has become a "constituent" of
the mourners of Diana, while her inner or "constituted" thoughts are

probably more on the passing out of history of an element of the British monarchy.

The film concludes with a scene in which the Queen confesses to Blair her deep distress at having disappointed many of her people. The emphasis here is on the painful process of adapting to the new situation that has left a lasting scar. Lacan describes this process as follows: "the formation of the I is symbolized in dreams by a fortress, or a stadium—its inner arena and enclosure, surrounded by marshes and rubbish-tips, dividing it into two opposed fields of contest where the subject flounders in quest of the lofty, remote inner castle" (*Ecrits*, 5). Refusing the protection of the castle and the limousine, the Queen decides to wander among her subjects outside, where she discovers an alien world: her people have changed and she is expected to adapt to that change. In short, she has discovered the impermanence of her own identity and later warns the Prime Minister that he too will be subject to the same force, a view, as we have seen, borne out by history. For, in Lacanian terms, the Queen and the Prime Minister, like the rest of us, are the subjects of discourse. There can be no permanence of identity for anyone.

This position is understandably controversial for psychologists and psychoanalysts, because it calls into question the assumption of an inner identity, a core ego that is essential to our being. However, Lacan's position implies that literary characters are not different in kind from "real people." Both are products of discourse, although the world we live in is not, so far as we know, created for artistic purposes. Literary characters cease to be entities in themselves and become agents of discourse, parts of a literary system, like images and symbols. In this respect Lacan is heavily influenced by the structuralists of the mid-twentieth century who, following in the footsteps of Ferdinand de Saussure, insisted that language should be understood not as a representation or linguistic picture of "reality" but as a system that requires decoding before it can be applied to "reality." Lacan uses the following anecdote to illustrate this point:

> A train arrives at a station. A little boy and little girl, brother and sister, in a compartment face to face next to the window through which the buildings along the station platform can be seen passing as the train pulls to a stop. "Look," says the brother, "we're at Ladies!": "Idiot," replies his sister, "Can't you see we're at Gentlemen?" (*Ecrits*, 167).

The only difference between the images that the brother and sister see is in the words "Ladies" and "Gentlemen," since the doors on which they appear are otherwise presumably identical. In this way, Lacan demonstrates that language is not a picture of reality but a code that needs to be deciphered before one can see "reality." However, Lacan's innovation is in adapting Saussure's concept to the unconscious in the daring assertion that the unconscious is language: "what the psychoanalytic experience discovers in the unconscious is the whole structure of language. Thus from the outset, the notion that the unconscious is merely the seat of the instincts will have to be rethought" (*Ecrits*, 163).

The unconscious as language: "The Reader"

What Lacan means by the unconscious as language is illustrated by "The Reader" (2008), directed by Stephen Daldry, with Kate Winslet as Hanna Schmitz, a part for which she received an Academy Award for Best Actress. Michael Berg as a young man is played by David Kross and as an adult by Ralph Fiennes. Set in Berlin in the 1950s, the film begins with the relationship between Hanna, a tramcar conductor, and Michael, a 15-year-old student. Becoming violently ill while returning home from school, Michael is helped by Hanna, a stranger, who kindly sees that he finds his way home. After Michael recovers from his illness, he calls on Hanna to thank her for helping him when he was unwell, and a sexual relationship begins. On a regular basis they have sex, then Michael reads to Hanna from his schoolbooks. He does not, however, learn about her wartime activities or that she is illiterate until many years later. This early period of their relationship is for both of them relatively happy except for a few instances when Hanna inexplicably loses her temper and is rude and unkind to Michael. The events that set off these eruptions of temper appear to be mere pretexts for a kind of anger that Hanna herself seems not to understand. For example, on one occasion, Michael goes to the tram to see Hanna, but she refuses to speak to him. Later, back at her home, she flares out at Michael because he was in the second-class compartment and she was in the first. When he complains that she does not realize that he took a great deal of time and effort to arrange the meeting, she heatedly tells him to leave and that he does not matter to her. In tears, Michael apologizes and begs for forgiveness, a pattern that occurs often enough that he later remarks that he always apologizes and she never does.

Lacan explains this kind of behavior by way of the term "aggressivity," which means the tendency toward aggression that is only occasionally expressed, remaining for the most part repressed:

> This aggressive intention is manifest: we constantly observe it in the formative aspect of an individual on those dependent upon him: intended aggressivity gnaws away, undermines, disintegrates; it castrates; it leads to death. "And I thought you were impotent," growled a mother, suddenly transformed into a tigress, to her son, who, with great difficulty had admitted to her his homosexual tendencies (*Ecrits*, 12).

This "tigress" mother reminds us of Hanna wounding the young Michael by asserting that he is incapable of upsetting her because she does not care about him. Lacan explains that the source of aggressivity relates to the concept of the imago, to be discussed in detail later in this chapter. Here, it is sufficient to keep in mind that Lacan uses this term to describe the self emerging from its protective cocoon:

> After the repeated failures of classical psychology to account for these mental phenomena [forms of aggressivity] [...] psychoanalysts made the first successful attempts to operate at the level of the concrete reality that they represent. This was because they set out from their formative function in the subject, and revealed that if the transient images determined such individual inflexions of the tendencies, it is as variations of the matrices that those other specific images, which we refer to by the term *imago*, are constituted for the "instincts" themselves (*Ecrits*, 12).

Lacan's analysis suggests to us that Hanna is struggling with a self that is emerging into a strange and alien world. Moreover, Lacan explains, it is no coincidence that this process undergone by Hanna is initiated by a sexual encounter. We recall that Hanna first notices Michael being aroused by watching her dress. Later, standing behind him naked in the bath, feeling his erect penis, she remarks, "that's why you came back." Sexual attraction and arousal occasioned by the arousal of the other are two key components of this procedure:

> It is in this erotic relation, in which the human individual fixes upon himself an image that alienates him from himself, that are to be found the energy and the form on which this organization of the passions that he will call his ego is based. This form will crystallize in the subject's conflictual internal tension, which determines the awakening of his desire for the object of the other's desire (*Ecrits*, 21).

This analysis seems very apt given Hanna's past. But at this early point in the film, young Michael has no idea that Hanna is illiterate. The audience begins to get a glimpse of her problem when she is particularly uncomfortable looking at a menu. Hiding her illiteracy out of shame is clearly a source of frustration which is one of the causes of her occasional eruptions of anger, but we subsequently learn that Hanna has a much deeper problem, one that lurks in her unconscious, undecipherable to her until she is able to read and write.

The movie now moves to Michael as a young adult in law school, who seems to be thriving academically but having problems in his social life. His love for Hanna perhaps lingers in his unconscious, which may explain in part why he is utterly devastated to discover that Hanna was a concentration camp guard. After Hanna has testified in court that she wrote the report about the women left to die in a burning church, Michael confesses to his law professor that he has information vital to the trial, for he now realizes that Hanna is illiterate and could not have written the report. The professor of course tells Michael that he is obliged to inform the court of anything relevant to the case. But here we confront Michael harboring shame reminiscent of that of Hanna. While she cannot reconcile herself to admitting to illiteracy, he refuses to talk to Hanna or inform the court of her illiteracy because it would implicate him in a personal relationship with her. And for both Hanna and Michael the means of getting in touch with their unconscious is by way of language. Hanna learns to read and write while in prison by comparing the tapes of Michael's readings with the books in the library. And Michael speaks about his relationship with Hanna, but only after she is dead. During over two decades of prison time Michael never writes or speaks to Hanna. Instead of replying to her letters, he sends cassettes of him reading. And near the end when they meet for the first time in nearly thirty years a few days before her release, she states her preference for his reading over her own, recognizing that those days are past.

In the next scene we learn that Hanna has committed suicide and left a will with instructions that Michael take all her savings to one of the two women who survived the church fire. By this means Hanna is showing us that in learning to read and write she has accepted responsibility for her acts as a guard and understood why Michael was unable to speak or write to her for nearly three decades. Hanna's shame has become guilt, whether that results from an understanding of Michael's view of her or from answering her own question to the judge, "What would you have done?", or both. The movie suggests that shame was Hanna's mechanism for repressing her guilt, leaving it dormant in her unconscious, and that she finally came to read, literally and figuratively, her unconscious, leading her to suicide.

Michael's shame turns to responsibility after the death of Hanna. First, as bidden in Hanna's will, he takes her money to the only survivor of the fire that is still alive. This woman insists that she be told the whole story, resulting in Michael telling for the first time, as he admits, of his early love relationship with Hanna. Then in the final scene of the film Michael takes his daughter to the grave of Hanna and recounts the story of his relationship with her. Since his daughter seems to be the only person alive whom he loves, his confession to her is not only an acceptance of responsibility but also, and more importantly, an attempt to explain and understand his love for Hanna.

At the end of the film we are left to confront a difficult problem. Why is it entitled "The Reader"? Why does it matter that Hanna has become a reader? When Michael explains to the last survivor of the fire that he only

discovered Hanna's illiteracy after their relationship had ended, she asks if
that excuses her behavior. Michael responds with a "no" that speaks for
all of us. So why should we care that Hanna has become literate? After all,
becoming a reader does not seem to make life more livable for Hanna. In
fact, it may even contribute to her suicide. Reading is what she associates
with Michael, and she recognizes that her favorite form of it, his reading
to her, is over. From early on, reading had been an important element of
their relationship, but at a certain point it changed. In the beginning they
first had sex and then Michael read to her. But then Hanna announced that
the order was to be reversed: the "kid" was to read first. Reading became a
form of love that prepared them for its physical manifestation. After initial
attraction, reading became their means of falling in love.

Indeed, Hanna's desire to read is an attempt to internalize Michael's
voice as a reader; in a sense, to climb into his brain. And perhaps that
is what leads, in the words of the prison warden, to her letting herself
go during her last few years, presumably the time after she was able to
read and write. Lacan remarks that "the unconscious of the subject is the
discourse of the other" (*Ecrits*, 61). Did Hanna come to understand why
Michael was ashamed of his relationship with her? Is that what she means
in her will by the phrase, "tell Michael that I said hello"? Is reading for
Hanna the means by which she first really hears the voice of the other? And
does it therefore enable her to hear for the first time the voices of her victims
for so long embedded in her unconscious?

But then what about Michael, who has been a reader from the beginning
of the film? How are we to understand his process of self-reconciliation?
Again, the issue is language. His problem involves speech. Not until he
is challenged by the last survivor of the fire does he admit to his love of
Hanna. After that, he is able to tell the entire story to his daughter, no less
an act of love than his reading to Hanna. And what will his daughter gather
from his narrative? Will she condemn him for not investigating Hanna's
background to avoid being involved with someone who worked willingly
for the Nazis? Or will she accept that Michael behaved like a normal
15-year-old within the realm of discourse available to a young man in the
Germany of the 1950s?

The implication of Lacan's view of the discourse of the unconscious is
that basic morality, common decency, that which directs one to be suspicious of anyone who seems to have survived unscathed in Germany during
the Nazi period is not innate or natural but a function of culture, a concept
learned from discourse. Twenty years later, after studying law and growing
up in a German culture, Michael comes to comprehend that his country has
reached a new, post-Nazi stage. Like Michael, we are left to struggle with
our feelings toward Hanna, a woman we should despise but for whom,
with the help of Kate Winslet's brilliant portrayal, we feel some empathy.
Lacan cautions us that the unconscious, a rich source of guilt, is a language

that must be read to be understood. Once Hanna can read her unconscious, she does not shirk from responsibility, believing that she no longer deserves Michael's love. But in psychoanalysis this stage usually involves what, since Freud, is known as "transference," when the analysand transfers responsibility to the analyst. As we would expect, for Lacan, this procedure is distinctly discursive:

> We wish to avoid the trap [...] that the patient addresses to us. It carries a secret within itself [...]. "Take upon yourself," the patient is telling us, "the evil that weighs me down; but if you remain smug, self-satisfied, unruffled as you are now, you won't be worthy of hearing it" (*Ecrits*, 15).

The only person Hanna can speak to about her past is Michael, who ironically refuses because of his own shame, his own need for an interlocutor, a need he only confronts after Hanna's death. Perhaps that is why Michael bursts into tears in Hanna's prison cell.

Transference and "Frost/Nixon"

"Frost/Nixon" (2008), directed by Ron Howard, starring Michael Sheen as David Frost and Frank Langella as Richard Nixon, is a good example of the process of transference as modified by Lacan into a form of discourse. This film is itself about public discourse in the form of newspapers, television, White House tapes, and film. Its structure is that of documentary journalism: the action is regularly interrupted by retrospective comments from the newspaper reporter, television news researcher, and radio/television director who serve as advisers to David Frost. Their remarks together become a journalistic narrative reminding us that the historical event reenacted is discursive, a "tele-historical" event.

Like Hanna, Nixon is another example of unacknowledged culpability, but Nixon is far from illiterate. In 1977, when this film takes place, Nixon had resigned from office but had not admitted to any wrongdoing. And there is a striking irony in the fact that Nixon first admits guilt on television. After losing the gubernatorial race in California he announced that the media would not have "[Nixon] to kick around any more." And it is precisely for this reason that the BBC managers do not expect Nixon to consider Frost's offer seriously. Nixon accepts, however, for two reasons: money and the fact that Frost is not a journalist but something akin to a game show host, and so, Nixon assumes, no match for him. In all respects but one Nixon is right: Frost is out of his depth. But, as the BBC television/radio director points out, Frost knows television, a discursive medium where Nixon, as we know from the debates with Kennedy, is vulnerable.

Money is important to Nixon because he feels excluded from the upper echelons of society, which are in his view reserved for east-coast, ivy-league graduates. An undergraduate at Whittier College in California and a graduate student at Duke University, Nixon uses money as an alternative to "class" or "poshness." And his assumption that dueling with Frost will be easy money is borne out in the early interviews when Frost is continually outmaneuvered and dominated by Nixon, whose command of facts and rhetorical powers make him a clear winner. But they both know that the last interview, on Watergate, is the crucial one. Even before we reach this final stage Nixon begins to ease up with Frost, noticing and remarking upon the interviewer's Italian loafers and his reputation as a womanizer. Moreover, Nixon points out to Frost that both share Methodism and experiences as outsiders, Frost at Cambridge and Nixon among the Washington establishment.

On the night before the final interview Nixon, in an inebriated state, phones Frost and points out that tomorrow is do or die for both of them: for the first time Nixon is giving Frost equal billing, recognizing that if no confession or startling new information emerges on the following day Frost will be ruined, having invested his own money and reputation in this series of interviews. It will be recalled that during this phone conversation, Nixon, admitting that he has had a few drinks, rails against the eastern establishment, angrily asserting that he will fight on against them and defeat them with his money and political power. He also asserts that Frost is like him, someone who can never be accepted by the establishment but who nevertheless continues to strive for its recognition. Even when Frost replies that he does not know what "Mr. President" is talking about, Nixon refuses to accept his denial, continuing to rant on about his enemies. Later retaining no memory of this phone conversation, Nixon gives a clear indication that it erupted from his unconscious and was later repressed. On the morning of the final interview while waiting for the camera crew to get ready, Nixon asks a bizarre question, marking perhaps the only comical moment in the film: he inquires if Frost engaged in any "fornication" last night. Lacan locates libido or "jouissance" along with aggressivity as key factors in transference situations. And, of course, as with the analyst and analysand, so too with Nixon and Frost, the transference is what Lacan, as we have seen, calls a "trap," a ploy to implicate the other in guilt and wrong-doing. Finally this conversation also involves Nixon's bold assertion of ego, that in the ensuing duel no holds will be barred, with the unmistakable implication that he expects to win—itself an indication of self-doubt or, in Lacan's terms, "frustration."

For in this labour which he undertakes to reconstruct for *another*, he rediscovers the fundamental alienation that made him construct it like *another,* and which has always destined it to be taken from him by *another.*

This ego [...] is frustration in its essence. [...] frustration by an object [...] the more it is elaborated the more profound the alienation from his *jouissance.*

The aggressivity experienced by the subject at this point has nothing to do with the animal aggressivity of frustrated desire [...] [but of] the slave whose response to the frustration of his labour is a desire for death (*Ecrits*, 46).

The latter phrase is most apparent in Nixon's turning to drink, an attempt to escape the next day's verbal combat that he professes to welcome, particularly since the result is loss of memory, a form of oblivion. By contrast, Frost has in fact been up all night reviewing the facts, which will enable him to catch Nixon up on circumstances regarding Charles Colson, one of Nixon's aides. Taken aback, Nixon is forced to admit that there was a cover-up, but he defends himself by asserting that if the President does it, it is legal. Shocked, Frost asks whether Nixon is saying that the President is above the law. At this point Nixon's chief of staff, Jack Brennan, rushes in to stop the interview, but after a pause Nixon comes back and makes his famous confession, "I let the American people down." The process here is very revealing. Frost first asks Nixon if he is now willing to admit to any wrong-doing, that the people need to know, deserve to hear from him on that point. Somewhat surprised, Nixon replies, "What would you have me say?" Frost then drops his clipboard, his script in a sense, and becomes for Nixon the Nixon that he wants Nixon to be: as an experienced television personality, he shows or rehearses Nixon in this medium that disconcerts him. Then and only then does Nixon confess. In Lacanian terms, he has taken on the desire of the other as his own.

How does Frost achieve what no one else could do, bring Nixon to admit not merely misjudgment but also culpability? Lacan would suggest, I believe, that this media or discursive event that Nixon expected to involve only his prowess at speech-making, included other elements, from Italian loafers and Frost's latest glamorous girlfriend to discussions of Methodism, fornication, and university experiences. Fascinated by difference and drawn by similarity, Nixon reacts with Frost, at one point of aggressivity defending presidential authority and then noticing Frost's shock at the notion that the president is above the law. Nixon, as we have seen in the phone conversation, has convinced himself that he has much in common with Frost, something Frost himself, rather like an experienced analyst, is skeptical about. Nevertheless, Nixon is attracted to Frost as a glamorous, socially successful form of himself. Lacan explains the function of libido in this form as follows:

There is a structural crossroads here [...] to understand the nature of aggressivity in man and its relation with the formalism of the ego and his objects. It is in this erotic relation, in which the human individual fixes upon himself an image that alienates him from himself, that are to be found the energy and the form on which this organization of the passions that he will call his ego is based. This form will crystallize in the subject's conflictual internal tension, which determines the awakening of his desire for the object of the other's desire (*Ecrits*, 21).

Lacan's conceptions help explain the many puzzling elements in the conclusion of "Frost/Nixon." A key point in the last interview is when Frost asks about the "people." Nixon had been defending the cover-up by pointing to the political partisanship around him in Congress and the media. But that was in the inner Washington world, so that when Frost mentions the people Nixon is at first caught off balance, that is, the imago emerges from the Washington DC cocoon, sees the rest of the country and admits that he has let those people down. From that moment on, as the newspaper reporter/narrator points out—and it is important to note that the narrator is a journalist, a creature of the media or discourse—Nixon's face changes markedly, now swollen with self-loathing, and we are informed that Frost was applauded for having exposed Nixon in front of the largest television audience of that era. And for a moment Nixon almost achieves tragic stature, acknowledging that he alone bears responsibility and will do so for the rest of his life, or, in the words of the narrator, that henceforth all great political scandals shall be known as "gates" after Watergate. We note that, in Lacanian terms, the imago has moved from the cocoon of the mirror stage to the next stage, the symbolic stage, the term Lacan uses for understanding the realm of discourse. Instead of blaming the media, Nixon's term for discourse, Nixon for the first time accepts responsibility for Watergate. Lacan describes this procedure as follows:

If it is to him that you have to speak, it is literally of something else, that is, of something other than that which is in question when he speaks of himself, and which is the thing that speaks to you, a thing which, whatever he says, would remain forever inaccessible to him, if in being speech addressed to you it could not elicit its response in you, and if, from having heard its speech in this inverted form, you could not, by returning it to him, give him the double satisfaction of having recognized it and of making him recognize its truth (*Ecrits*, 144).

So, hearing Nixon's refusal to "grovel," Frost cleverly provides for him a dignified, almost tragic confession, giving Nixon the double satisfaction of having recognized it as less than totally demeaning but nevertheless as the truth.

Yet the film does not end there. Frost visits Nixon at his San Clemente, California home before leaving for London. Nixon cordially invites Frost and his girlfriend to tea, congratulates Frost on the vast audience and the pro-Frost anti-Nixon reviews. But he is not surprised, as the "sons of whores" have always been out to get him, indicating that Nixon's imago has retreated back into the cocoon of paranoia. Nonetheless, he charmingly apologizes to Frost's female companion for swearing, remarking, in a rare moment of humor, that he would have said "sons of bitches" but that his servant is very fond of dogs. Then he graciously accepts Frost's gift of a pair of Italian loafers, clearly moved, somehow losing sight of the fact that Frost is a part, perhaps the most lethal part, of the journalistic establishment that he believes has ruined him. On the contrary, Nixon is fascinated by Frost, asks him in private if he enjoys his parties, admits envy of his happiness and confesses that he is unsuitable to be a politician because not at ease with people. We return then to the two key Lacanian elements: discourse, "what about the people?" and libido, Nixon's attraction to Frost's enjoyment of people, particularly beautiful women.

Lastly, remembering nothing of the phone conversation on the evening before the final interview, Nixon asks Frost what they discussed. Frost replies "cheeseburgers." But that is only partially accurate; Frost kindly refrains from embarrassing "Mr. President" about his angry rant. But in that conversation, Nixon had confronted the otherness of himself in Frost, saying that both of their reputations were on the line, with the stakes much the same for both. But that moment when Nixon entered the world of other people, Frost and "the American people," has now passed without memory. And we in the audience are left with what Nixon calls the media and Lacan calls discourse playing its final trick on "tricky Dick." For we witness the visual record of Nixon retreating into his shell, relegating his moment with the people into his unconscious, which may help explain how the only man who ever resigned the U.S. presidency lived on after these interviews, as the movie informs us, for 17 years.

So while his enemies celebrate, Nixon carries on for almost two more decades. What are we to conclude from this fact? Could the man who took responsibility for attempting to fix an election and was forced to resign the presidency for it, live with this guilt for 17 years? Or could he have decided that, once again, the media selected him as the convenient scapegoat, the object of scorn, instead of admiring him for carrying on his shoulders the sins of his loyal aides? Is the concept of an innate ego, beyond the tentacles of discourse, merely an illusion that allows us to bear the battering of the media in Nixon's case, a necessary illusion for survival? Is the "imago" that emerges out of the mirror stage into the symbolic realm of discourse the hard core of our ego or does it evolve into something different, an identity that has historical continuity but no essence?

Imago and "Lost in Translation"

To consider this Lacanian question I turn to the film "Lost in Translation" (2003), directed by Sofia Coppola and starring Bill Murray as Bob Davis and Scarlett Johansson as Charlotte. Bob and Charlotte travel separately to Tokyo, first meeting in a hotel bar where they share the experience of sleeplessness and jet lag. Soon they become friends because of their desire to leave Tokyo that for both evokes feelings of disorientation and loneliness. Bob must remain to complete his lucrative contract for a whisky advertisement, and Charlotte cannot leave until her husband completes his photography assignment. The first question raised by the film is why are these two very different people, a young, recently married college graduate and a middle-aged actor married for 25 years, ill at ease in Tokyo, despite being provided every comfort and convenience in a luxurious, well appointed hotel with impeccable service. The film very adroitly communicates to the audience, in my view, the discomfort of the characters by displaying Tokyo as a sort of karaoke city. It is thoroughlyWesternized and up-to-date with almost everything one could find in New York or Los Angeles, except that the language and customs are very different. As the taxi arrives in Tokyo from the airport, we see a mass of gaudy neon signs that are all incomprehensible to those with only Western languages: the problem is compounded by the fact that Japanese, like many Eastern languages, is syllabic not alphabetical, so one cannot even try to read the signs letter by letter in the way that most of us can struggle with Greek or Russian. Still more disconcerting is that, unlike foreign European cities that are marked by architecture that is distinct to their various cultures, Tokyo, at least the part of the city that we see, is all contemporary glass and steel, a sort of computer-game city, anywhere and nowhere. Bob and Charlotte are disoriented by a radical change in discourse, a discourse that is as all-encompassing and constricting as a cocoon. In fact, at one point, Bob only half jokingly says to Charlotte he is organizing a prison break and invites her to join in, eliciting her immediate positive response.

The "break-out" from the cocoon is accomplished, as Lacan would have predicted, by the libido, their attraction to one another. And together they tackle the new discourse, taking Charlotte to the emergency room for medical treatment, then going out to a restaurant and meeting some of the locals at a party. But we see them separately before they come together, and each in their different ways shows an openness to the new culture. When Bob first arrives at the hotel where various officials of the hotel address him in Japanese and, to his surprise, hand him gifts, Bob, with characteristic humor, quips that they all look tired with jet lag and need to get some sleep. On the first day of her arrival, Charlotte goes off on her own to visit a religious shrine. But nonetheless they both want to leave as soon as possible, until they meet one another.

Indeed, Bob extends his stay so that he can see more of Charlotte, and appears as a guest on a Japanese television show, one of the funniest and most bizarre scenes of the movie. The zany television host speaks no English and Bob of course has no Japanese, yet the "interview" seems to work because, as a seasoned actor, Bob picks up what is required by way of body language and gesture. He is somehow treading water in a strange new sea that involves not just language but all the mental stimuli of a culture. At one point the host, whose gender is somewhat ambiguous, asks Bob to dance. With controlled California casualness, Bob good-naturedly participates, much to the glee of the clown-like host. Similarly, Charlotte wanders down to the lobby to hear an American starlet tell her fans about her interest in elements of Japanese culture. But it is clear from her presentation and her previous conversation that this woman is not interested in anything other than herself. So Charlotte wanders into another room where a number of Japanese women in traditional dress are involved in flower arrangement: the organizer of this group, apparently assuming that Charlotte wishes to participate, starts her off with a bouquet and Charlotte acquiesces, amused and somewhat interested.

Bob and Charlotte are, the film makes plain at the outset, both open to this new culture but profoundly put off by it in ways that neither of them understands. Lacan suggests that we see here a shared element of the unconscious:

> The subject goes well beyond what is experienced "subjectively" by the individual, exactly as far as the truth he is able to attain [...] Yes, this truth of his history is not all contained in his script, and yet the place is marked there by the painful shocks he feels from knowing only his own lines (*Ecrits*, 61).

Here we are reminded of Bob at the shooting of the whisky commercial. We first notice that the Japanese director speaks volubly and at length to Bob, but the translation is terse and polite. At first, Bob asks if that is all he was saying, but then he becomes accustomed to accepting that much is lost in translation and that, given the director's seeming passion and temper, this is perhaps a blessing. But the gap or chasm between the original Japanese and the translation is a kind of cultural abyss that reinforces disorientation and unease. This gap is accentuated when the director resorts to English, "OK?" he says to Bob, who replies, in tranquil puzzlement, "OK." The two letters suddenly take on a wholly different meaning, as if only coincidentally the same but from different languages. Charlotte has a similar experience at the religious shrine. We recognize that something solemn and spiritual is happening but are completely unable to grasp what it is. As Bob and Charlotte converse, their interest, puzzlement, alienation and fascination come to the fore. At one point Charlotte asks Bob whether he will be staying on, eliciting the reply that, yes, he will be at the bar for the next few days, humorously communicating how she also feels.

Gradually, Bob and Charlotte begin to navigate outside the hotel, meeting in various places and "conversing" in a way with the Japanese, a development that brings them closer to one another, until near the end we see them lying in bed together, fully clothed but in a quite intimate conversation. He gives her rather reassuring fatherly advice about her future, and, when the next morning she appears at his hotel, she is aware of another woman there with whom he has spent the night. Can we thus assume that Bob's relationship with Charlotte was only friendship, not involving sexual attraction or love? The end does not satisfactorily resolve this question. Bob waits in the lobby to say goodbye, but their parting is cordial, nothing more. Then Bob sees her through the window of the car taking him to the airport, and orders the driver to stop. He embraces and kisses her, and whispers something in her ear that we never hear—something else lost in translation—which causes her eyes to brim with tears. He leaves her, walking backwards, smiling fondly. Is the secret between them kept from us because you had to be there to understand? Have they experienced a sharing of the discourse of the unconscious, of the cultural gap from which we in the audience are at one remove?

The film, in my view, leaves us with the same doubts that the characters themselves probably feel, as to what did happen. Did they fall in love or was it merely the momentary friendship of two disoriented people sharing their isolation? The change in discourse changed them: whether temporarily or permanently is an open question. Is the ego that draws Charlotte back to her husband and Bob back to his family really somewhere deep in their psyches or an illusion that permits them to maintain their sense of selfhood in a world, especially in one marked by easy access to exotic places, of alien yet familiar discourses? That question will, I suspect, remain in dispute. But Lacan teaches us that our selfhood, our identity, is in the thrall of discourse— whether permanently or momentarily—and that lack of awareness of this fact dooms us like the Nixon of "Frost/Nixon" to forever repeat the stage of imago, reemerging from the cocoon to the symbolic realm of discourse and mistaking it for the "real." Lacan shows us that the self is like a character in literature, a creature of a context called discourse, and that understanding that self requires the ability to interpret the context, to understand our place in the discourse, even if the effect of that context is only temporary.

"L'Auberge espagnole" and "The King's Speech"

A recent film that points to the relationship between the elements of Lacan considered in this chapter is Cédric Klapisch's "L'Auberge espagnole"

(2002), translated as "Pot Luck," starring Audrey Tautou and Romain Duris. Born and bred in Paris, Xavier decides to live in Barcelona for a year in order to learn Spanish, a requirement for a job. As an Erasmus scholar enrolled in university he cannot afford to live alone, so he boards first with friends of his mother, then with some recent acquaintances, until he is finally accepted as a housemate in an international apartment including speakers of Danish, English (British), Spanish, Catalan, German, Italian, and French (Belgian). Although studying economics, he is educated more profoundly by the various languages and cultures of his housemates. In fact, Xavier's sense of his identity is radically altered by his confrontation with these foreign tongues, as the notion of the "mirror stage" would suggest. At first he appears to be a typical young Frenchman, very serious about his studies, devoted to his girlfriend in Paris, and not interested in socializing with the others. Gradually, however, he acclimatizes to the Spanish way of life and becomes a lively participant and lover of the party atmosphere of the "auberge." In fact on one occasion he insists that Wendy, the young British woman, should stop working all of the time and go out to the bar with the rest of the group. And Wendy changes as a result of this experience, becoming more outgoing with her housemates, eventually having a sexual relationship with an American. Indeed, the social world of this film, particularly the parties, is always richly textured with languages, or more accurately discourses. For although the setting is almost exclusively Barcelona the students bring their own cultures to bear upon the Spanish scene. This mixture is what Xavier particularly enjoys. And part of the pleasure is that this atmosphere exposes unconscious desires: Wendy, the rather uptight British woman, admits that her attraction to the American is purely sexual, and Xavier learns from his lesbian housemate how to woo the wife of an acquaintance.

The libido, as Lacan predicted, leads the way toward new discursive experiences; language learning involves comprehending cultural conventions, from economics to sex. On the occasion of a surprise visit from the landlord, Xavier's new ability with Spanish saves the day. Disgusted at the mess, the landlord orders them out of the apartment. Xavier reasons with him, and eventually he relents, but only after insisting that he now deals exclusively with Xavier. By contrast, Xavier's affair with the married woman begins when he criticizes her for being intolerant of Spanish society; ironically, she thus becomes more attracted to him, envying his integration with Catalan culture. In Lacanian terms, she is attracted to the desire of the other.

But new pleasures occasion new pains. We see the agony of people coming to grips with the price one pays for acting upon desires that had hitherto remained repressed. The wife of the neurosurgeon whom Xavier had seduced returns to her boring marriage. And Wendy's brother has to pretend to be gay in order to prevent her British boyfriend discovering her in bed with her American lover. Our cultures of origin require the repression of certain pleasures that are permissible in other cultures. In fact, Xavier's fascination with other cultures is because of a sense of frustration with home. He is often angry ("aggressivity") with his mother, the source of his mirror stage, for reasons he cannot explain or understand until he leaves France and acts in ways he knows his mother would not condone. Not surprisingly, the new self that emerges in a foreign country is at once liberating and frightening. Transference is one symptom of this experience. The most vivid illustration in the film is when Xavier transfers his guilt about his extramarital affair to the wife's husband, the neurosurgeon. Depressed and sleep-deprived, Xavier turns to her husband for a physiological solution; after tests, the doctor tells Xavier that he is well physically but must stay away from his wife who has confessed all to him. The concept of the imago is seen at the end of the film when Martine, Xavier's Parisian girlfriend, admits that she lied to him about having another lover. Xavier tells us that he has decided to end this relationship. Why? Martine was toying with him, but Xavier, although disloyal to Martine, was not playing a game. What happened to Xavier and his housemates was serious, the result of their attempts to understand, cope with, and live in a new environment. And in the end Xavier has a new sense of himself. He has grown beyond the self that loved Martine and can now smile at and tolerate his mother. His mother and Martine have remained unchanged in Paris. Perhaps the world that Xavier sees for himself is no more real or genuine than that of Martine and his mother, but Lacan's insight, I believe, is a warning about what discourse does to us and that we need to understand and adapt to that phenomenon.

The most recent film to exemplify Lacan's concepts is "The King's Speech" (2011), directed by Tom Hooper, starring Colin Firth, Geoffrey Rush, and Helena Bonham Carter. Early in the film, when King George V points to the microphone of the "wireless," warning that that object will make the royals into "actors," we are in the presence of the problem of discourse. The King's assertion may be an originary myth but it enables the film to announce its subject: namely that royal influence at this stage of history takes the form of a voice on the "wireless." At first, the Duke and Duchess of York try to maintain that his speech problem is merely mechanical. But it soon becomes clear that the source of the problem is psychological. In fact, it seems to go back to a very early period of his life. We learn that in infancy he had a cruel nanny, that at a very early stage he was punished for being left-handed, and that his legs were set in braces to correct their alignment. By the time he was four or five years of age, his brothers made fun of him by imitating his stutter, and the King encouraged them to do so in the belief that it would cure the young Duke. But of course quite the opposite was the result; Bertie accepted the family mirror image of him as his self-image or identity, and the stammer remained the hallmark of his personality. In the early period when Bertie was emerging from the imaginary realm of the mirror stage to the symbolic one of discourse, he was constricted and restrained.

As a result, he is a deeply frustrated man, subject to bouts of aggressivity that occur in the form of anger or dismissal whenever reference is made to his early personal life, for that is when the imago trying to emerge was punished and restricted. The turning point of the film is when he loses his temper with his speech therapist, Lionel Logue. During a conversation about Bertie's relationship with his older brother, Lionel tells the Duke he will make an excellent king. Ironically, Bertie for the first time adopts the posture of an authoritarian aristocrat with Logue, angrily denouncing him as a commoner and dismissing him from his presence with an hauteur worthy of King Lear. Of course, the anger here, as Logue realizes in retrospect, is the result of fear. The imago retreats back into the nursery/cocoon rather than face the possibility of a place in the symbolic, discursive world as king.

But the stammer that vanished in the moment of pitched anger soon returns. For Bertie resists the king within himself because his single consolation for his speech impediment is the assumption that he will at least never be burdened with the responsibility of being on the throne. As the Duchess confesses to him, she refused his proposal of marriage twice not because she did not love him but because of her hesitation about the public service required of members of the royal family. She goes on to explain that she accepted in the end, believing that with his stammer they would be left for the most part to their private life. When historical circumstances force the Duke into public prominence, he turns back to Logue, apologizes for his outburst and engages in serious therapy.

Logue probes the discourse of Bertie's unconscious, focusing on body language and speech. Profanity, something forbidden in the royal family, is let loose, allowing Bertie to have moments of fluent speech. As he gains self-confidence and begins to trust Logue, he confides in him about one of his father's last remarks: "Bertie has more guts than all of the rest of his brothers put together," an insight borne out by the film. In the end "guts" and language combine to make King George VI. Finding a voice involves relating to others, making a friend of Lionel, entering a social system which, according to Lacan, is like language, a realm that permits some maneuverability, some individuality, but with clear parameters, rules and conventions. At one point, the Archbishop of Canterbury threatens to replace Logue, but Bertie refuses to allow it. When the Archbishop justifies his decision by explaining that he has the duty to protect the head that he is about to crown, Bertie deftly replies, without a stammer, "that is my head." Authority and voice arise in protecting a friend, as Bertie now refers to Lionel. When speech for Bertie is a functional act in a social context, he seldom stutters.

The title of the film and the prominence of the speech therapist—and Geoffrey Rush received almost as many nominations for the Academy Award as did Colin Firth and Helena Bonham Carter—testify to the importance of discourse, to its psychological ramifications. With the help of Logue, Bertie comes to recognize that to be the leader of his people he must establish his own voice, which is seen in Lacanian terms in this film as involving finding his place in public discourse. For example, at the coronation, Bertie insists that Lionel be seated with his family, a sign of affection, since Bertie is only truly at ease with his family, where he shows love and devotion for his wife and two daughters. Including Lionel in that inner sanctum is a sign of mediation between the imaginary cocoon and the symbolic public world, a bridge between family and society.

The end of "The King's Speech" provides an apt conclusion for this chapter. King George VI completes his longest and most important public address with a good degree of fluency and dignity. Logue points out that he only stumbled over the "w's" and the King replies that he threw those in so they would know it was him. Humor about himself, particularly in the form of verbal deftness, enhances his self-esteem. We see the BBC radio technicians applauding him as he leaves the studio. Colin Firth brilliantly demonstrates that, although the speech succeeds as an oration, the delivery required a supreme effort. In short, King George VI first achieves the stature of a king by way of oratory, by showing his subjects his determination to master the form of discourse crucial to his position, public speaking. In that respect, he is a Lacanian king. Colin Firth received the Academy Award for Best Actor in his role as King George VI, a reward, in my view, he well deserved. But is it perhaps a sign of our time that the hero of the present is a discourse-king?

Lacan's innovative ideas are of immediate importance to the individual. The next chapter considers groups of people. Fredric Jameson reexamines how literary analysis relates to the social and political structures of our culture.

CHAPTER FIVE

Post-Marxism, Fredric Jameson

Summary: *The chapter begins by explaining that Jameson's innovation is in establishing a distinction between the inner and outer form of artworks. The first section addresses how to analyze form, or hermeneutics, illustrated by "Goodbye Lenin." Inner form is introduced by way of the music of "Il Postino." In the next section, "The Lives of Others" helps explain how Hegel's notion of individual consciousness is the source of inner form. The relationship for Jameson between Hegel and Marx is considered in the analysis of "The Constant Gardener." The dialectic of individual consciousness and economic history, the focal point of inner and outer form, is exemplified in "Invictus." The coda is a brief analysis of "Made in Dagenham" which makes overt a distinction between inner and outer form.*

Fredric Jameson's contribution to literary theory is the distinction between the inner and outer form of artworks. By this means Jameson deconstructs the old or what he calls the "vulgar" Marxist view that considers only the outer form that is apparent without interpretive analysis. Inner form, by contrast, requires attention to the purpose of the individual text and involves "hermeneutics" or interpretation. By this means we shall see, in the conclusion, Jameson's innovation provides an insight into how acts of individual integrity are not merely swallowed up in the larger social and political movements but can make an important contribution within a Marxist framework, that is, to history.

Hermeneutics and "Goodbye Lenin"

Jameson explains inner form by considering hermeneutics:

> [...]inner form, is [...] a *hermeneutic* concept, that is, it does not imply a
> truth of a positivistic kind somehow timelessly associated with its object,
> like the laws of the natural sciences; rather, it emphasizes the operation
> of interpretation itself, as it moves in time from outer to inner form as
> from one moment to another in a dialectical process. Thus the critic is
> recalled to his own procedures, as a form unfolding in time but also
> reflecting his own concrete social and historical situation (*Marxism and
> Form*, 401).

A good illustration of this distinction between inner and outer form can be
seen in "Goodbye Lenin," released in 2003, directed by Wolfgang Becker
and starring Daniel Brühl as Alex Kerner. The outer form of this film might
be described as follows. A German family separated by the Berlin Wall is,
after the fall of the Wall, brought back together. Although the mother is
dying and the father has children with another woman, the reassembling of
this family is a microcosm of the reunification of Germany, which, although
fraught with problems, is seen as an improvement over the previous
situation of separation and alienation. Focusing upon this outer form, the
"vulgar Marxist," to use Jameson's phrase, might be tempted to interpret
the movie as heralding the triumph of West Germany over East Germany,
of capitalism over communism. But an analysis of inner form leads to a very
different conclusion.

Examining the film in greater detail, we become aware of a dialectic
involving points of view. In the prologue, Alex, a young boy living in East
Germany before the fall of the Wall, explains how proud he was in 1978
when an East German was the first German cosmonaut to be launched
into space. The movie concludes with Alex launching his mother's ashes
into the air by way of a rocket. In the body of the film, Alex, now an adult
and after the fall of the Wall, takes a taxi to visit his father in West Berlin.
He recognizes the cab driver as the cosmonaut who had years earlier been
his role model. Now one of the heroes of communist East Germany drives
Alex to West Germany. In Alex's past the cosmonaut by his example had
encouraged the young boy to look up, to see his dull, drab life on earth from
the new and exciting perspective of space. By contrast, the cosmonaut's taxi
ride suggests a different perspective: instead of the vertical earth–space axis,
we take a horizontal ride between East and West Berlin.

This crossing of perspective axes signals that the film is not content with
the usual contrast between the two sides of divided Berlin. In Jameson's
terms, we are "recalled to our own procedures," alerting us to be skeptical

about the old dichotomy of West versus East, since our "own concrete and historical situation" is situated after the unification of Berlin. The double perspective suggested by this interpretation keeps both the horizontal and vertical axes in mind; we see at once the East–West contrast and the view from above a unified Germany. This hermeneutic framework gives a new shape to the content of the film. Jameson describes the relationship between form and content as follows:

> [Form and content have] a relationship of identity which nonetheless requires a complete translation from one set of terms into the other: the two dimensions are one and indeed the propaedeutic value of art lies in the way in which it permits us to grasp the essentially historical and social value of what we had otherwise taken to be a question of individual experience. Yet this is done by shifting levels or points of view, by moving from the experience to its ground or concrete situation, as from a form to a content or from a content to a form (*Marxism and Form*, 407).

Now we can reconsider the film in relation to the cross-perspective form. Alex's father escaped to the West, becoming a prosperous doctor but leaving his mother and two children in the East, living, as we would expect, in a much less luxurious fashion. Near the end, we discover that he has, in fact, not deserted his family. Rather, the plan was for the mother to follow him to the West with the family, but she never tried to escape, fearing that if caught she would lose her children. Alex and his sister, who had been led by their mother to believe that their father left them behind for a life of luxury and another woman, come to realize that for three years he waited for them and wrote them letters, hidden by the mother, indicating his love and continued concern for them. The children have been deceived by their mother into believing that their father is an irresponsible capitalist. Alex and his sister are thus disabused of the view of their father within the old dichotomy: selfish, individualistic capitalism versus collective, communal communism. The source of this dichotomy is of course East German government propaganda that we see in the form of a military parade and an award ceremony for workers who value the community over individual gain. The latter becomes prominent because Alex's mother is one of the recipients. By this means the public and private come together, an important element of Jameson's concept of inner form.

> The terms in which we describe this inner form [...] are however less important than the movement itself, by which we reemerge into that *place of the concrete* which has been described [...] as the mediation between public and private, between individual and socio-economic realities, between the existential and history itself (*Marxism and Form*, 406).

The private deception of her children by Christiane, Alex's mother, is aided by the public propaganda of the East German government. Alex learns of this relationship and shows us precisely how it operates when he sets about deceiving his mother into believing that the Berlin Wall has not fallen and that East Germany remains a viable state. Alex's existential reality, the need to hide from his mother the fall of the wall, reveals in historical terms how the East German government lulled its population into believing that it was defeating the West.

To prevent his mother having another heart attack, Alex decides to recreate the world that is familiar to her, that of East Germany before the fall of the Wall. With the help of his Russian friend Dennis, a technological whiz, and the rest of the family, Alex recreates in his mother's bedroom the mundane and routine reality of communist East Germany. And because this process requires the removal of the Western-style redecorating that occurred since the wall was dismantled and Christiane was in hospital, we see in precise detail the quotidian differences between everyday existence in the East and the West.

A further function of this process is that instead of the usual viewpoint of the West looking at the East, we are placed in the East looking westward, that is, seeing ourselves from the point of view of the other. And what we see from the East, I would suggest, is something quite different from what we would expect. For example, after the Wall comes down, Alex's job changes from repairing appliances and technical equipment, an occupation that we might now describe as green, to selling satellite TV aerials, a product that seems particularly out of place in a society with high unemployment and a very short supply of basic necessities. Another revealing moment is when Christiane begins to recover and ventures outside her apartment building. At first, seeing piles of furniture from the other apartments, she thinks that some people are moving, unaware that they are discarding their unfashionable décor. Then she notices expensive, large Western cars, and the audience feels that this sector of Berlin has been transformed into an American-style ghetto, a Detroit with its juxtaposition of shiny new cars on streets filled with the detritus of deprivation. Finally Christiane sees the statue of Lenin being towed away. Once Alex finds his mother and takes her back to the apartment, he decides to explain this spectacle by claiming that East Germany has, as an act of charity, opened its doors to desperate West Germans who are disillusioned with their way of life—a position that now from the perspective of the film seems much less far-fetched than we would have expected. We are left with the image of Lenin moving toward and pointing to the East, only now we wonder whether this striking image suggests not only the end of East German communism but also a major change in West German capitalism.

In place of the notion of the West triumphing over the East, we have a more complex view: the gains for the East from the West are obvious but thrown into new prominence is what has been lost, all the advantages of the tight social safety net that not only restricted freedom but also sustained Christiane's family and many others like them. When Alex at the end of the film sends his mother's ashes up into space and shows us pictures of her East German world now past, the point is not merely nostalgia. Like the age of chivalry, East German communism is relegated to the past, a way of life that in most respects but not all is well lost. And as we still maintain some remnants of chivalric courtesy in our society, so, too, the new "inner form" perspective of "Goodbye Lenin" suggests we would do well not to reject all elements of the sector of Berlin that lay on the other side of the Wall. The post-Marxist view of this film therefore could argue that instead of being a form of "bourgeois propaganda," or the West congratulating itself on its victory over the East, it is a warning about the complacency of such an attitude.

To summarize, the post-Marxist position on "Goodbye Lenin" suggests, in my view, that the East–West German rivalry is only the superficial topic of the film. The real concrete situation is the need to combine the best aspects of both sectors, both ideologies, to form a unified country that is a home for both East and West Germans. Here we see what Jameson describes as "the disguise and revelation of the concrete":

> If this suggests something of the way a Marxist criticism would reconstruct the inner form [...] as both disguise and revelation of the concrete, it remains for us to say a word about the implications of such a theory for judgment [...] as currently practiced. For to claim that the task of the critic is to reveal this censored dimension of the work implies precisely that, at least as art is practiced today, in the society in which it is practiced, the surface of the work is a kind of mystification in its structure (*Marxism and Form*, 413).

The discovery of inner form often involves, for Jameson, penetration beneath an artistic surface that is deceptive, like the picture of the world Christiane presents to her children and which ironically her children present to her. Hermeneutics involves piercing through the façade of external beauty or prettiness.

Musical inner form and "Il Postino"

Jameson further describes the complex notion of inner form or the microcosm in the context of music because it is the one art that separates itself from or has little relation to the other arts.

> So it is that western music at the very outset marks itself off from the culture as a whole, reconstitutes itself as a self-contained and

autonomous sphere at a distance from the everyday social life of the period and developing, as it were, parallel to it. Not only does music thereby acquire an internal history of its own, but it also begins to duplicate on a smaller scale all of the structures and levels of the social and economic microcosm itself, and displays its own internal dialectic, its own producers and consumers, its own infrastructure (*Marxism and Form*, 14).

In this way Jameson suggests that a microcosm has within its limited sphere a certain kind of independence. Hans Robert Jauss, whose position was discussed in Chapter Four, has explained this notion by using the image of the planets within our solar system. Each planet has its own orbit while being restricted by the larger forces of the constellation. The solar system ultimately controls its constellation and is itself subject to the larger forces in the larger cosmos. The planets are analogous to literary genres, the constellation is like the realm of the arts, and the solar system is equivalent to history.

An apt illustration of this notion is contained in the movie "Il Postino," released in 1994, directed by Michael Radford and starring Philippe Noiret as the famous Chilean poet Pablo Neruda, and Massimo Troisi as Mario the postman. Exiled from his native land because of his subversive poetry, Neruda is allowed by the Italian government to settle on a small island where a young man named Mario, desperate to escape the life of a fisherman, has just taken a job as a postman. The young postman soon becomes impressed with Neruda as a poet and lover. After falling in love with a young local woman he decides to ask Neruda to help him become a poet in order to woo his beloved. Eventually he succeeds, at least to the extent that his love poetry helps persuade Beatrice to accept his marriage proposal.

The theme song is a romantic, sweet yet melancholy and characteristically Italian melody: it received both an Academy and Bafta award for Best Soundtrack. A variation of it is heard in every scene when Mario rides his bike up to Neruda's house, the source of poetry and the language of love. Most of the film is punctuated with gentle, romantic music. There are, however, two notable exceptions. When Beatrice's mother comes to Neruda to complain of Mario's designs on her daughter, she interrupts the older couple dancing; once they see her the music stops. And again the music is replaced with the noise of anger when Neruda is annoyed by Mario's insistence that he write a poem for Beatrice. These two exceptions make clear that the main musical theme is associated with love and poetry.

By this means, Mario's love and Neruda's poetry take on the sort of autonomy that Jameson describes above. Indeed, the two scenes where the music stops or is absent are both moments when the inner integrity of the poetry or love is questioned and where we see the "parallel development"

Jameson describes. Beatrice's mother believes Mario has sexual designs on her daughter, but the postman's persistent and decorous courtship of Beatrice proves her wrong. Neruda objects to Mario's request for a poem about Beatrice because he has never seen or met her; poetry, he teaches Mario, is not made to order but at its best springs from inspiration. Later, as an act of friendship he accompanies Mario to the inn, meets Beatrice, and in her presence signs a dedication to his friend. Love and poetry each require different kinds of integrity, separate but parallel. But love and poetry are only a part of this film that is mainly concerned with politics, the cause of Neruda's exile and Mario's death. The relation between politics and poetry is again emphasized by the music. In the final scene of the film, when Neruda is listening to Mario dedicating his poem to him and imagining the death of the postman, the theme is heard in the background, now on the soft, mournful piano rather than the bright accordion.

Jameson describes the part–whole relationship with reference to music and philosophy:

> Just as the Beethoven sonata stood as the precarious synthesis of whole and part, so the philosophy of Hegel is one long tension between the overall organization of the dialectic, with Absolute Spirit as the end result of the process, and the individual moments, the steps of the dialectic, the concrete analysis of the various steps along the way. The two components depend upon each other and cannot be considered separately (*Marxism and Form*, 47).

While the parts of the film concerned with love and poetry develop by way of inner form, signaled by the musical motifs, they are subsumed by the larger whole that for the Marxist is always history. In the background during this courtship is an upcoming election. There is no source of potable water on the island. The ship that regularly delivers water to the island cannot provide enough for the whole population. One of the candidates running for office promises to remedy this situation, but when elected he fails to fulfill his promise. During the campaign but before the election, Neruda is allowed to return to Chile. Mario writes him many letters and even sends him a recording of the sounds of the island but does not receive a reply from the great poet. Perhaps the music of the island has now become only a small part of Neruda's life as an internationally recognized artist. As time passes Mario has a child, presumably becomes active in the Italian communist party, and seems to be known as the local poet since he is invited to recite from his works at a political party rally. We subsequently learn that at this rally during an altercation between the police and demonstrators, some people were killed, one of whom was Mario. Finally Neruda returns to the island—its music still a part of his life—and meets his namesake, Mario's son Pablito. When Mario's widow explains what has happened to Mario, Neruda begins to recreate the scene in his mind. The film concludes with Neruda walking along the beach where he and Mario often conversed about love and poetry—the now familiar musical refrain is again heard—while we are shown what Neruda is imagining. Called to speak at this great assembly, a sort of spiritual/poetic leader, Mario is swallowed up in the melée of what one character in the film calls *"il popolo,"* the people.

Mario was initially drawn to poetry for personal reasons, admiration for Neruda as an individual and an interest in using the art of what he calls *"metafore"* to express his love for Beatrice. But Neruda sees him as part of a social and political mass movement, an attempt to change the government in Italy. So we understand the dialectic of poetry as a semi-independent planet, enabling Mario to communicate his love to Beatrice. But Mario the poet is also subject to the larger forces of history, in this instance resulting in his death. Yet the film leaves us with both orbits, rather than either one or the other: little Pablito, the child of love poetry, and Mario's death, the result of poetry in the political arena. Neruda sees both aspects of poetry and presents the spectacle of the relationship to us, making clear how he can be simultaneously committed to poetry and to his friendship with Mario while using all of his creative powers to help overthrow Chilean authoritarianism.

And the movie itself, "Il Postino," is a form of poetry in the ancient sense of art, demonstrating that when poetry enters politics it is subject to—while having an effect upon—the larger forces of history. In this respect it is significant that the film is dedicated to Massimo Troisi, who played the part of the postman and died before the film was completed. Since Troisi was a well known actor of Italian farces, his death, like that of Mario as a budding poet, leads us to ask what for Post-Marxism is the function of the artist in the realm of socio-political forces beyond the control of any single person. For Jameson, inner form is the Hegelian part of the whole, the individual that he wishes to preserve in the Marxian system. At the end of "Il Postino" we are left with music and poetry as forces for change, but what of Mario's place in history? That question remains unanswered. Following in the footsteps of Neruda, Mario courageously devoted his poetry to the political cause, but we have no idea if his personal sacrifice in any way furthered the cause.

The role of the individual in history: "The Lives of Others"

"Il Postino" ended with a sad reminder of the question that is pursued in "The Lives of Others" ["Das Leben der Anderen"], released in 2006, directed by Florian Henckel von Donnersmarck and starring Ulrich Mühe as Stasi Captain Gerd Wiesler, Sebastian Koch as the playwright, Georg Dreyman, and Martina Gedeck as the actress, Christa-Maria Sieland. The issue alluded to at the end of "Il Postino" and raised at the beginning of "The Lives of Others" is the relationship between the individual and the state. In particular, "The Lives of Others" considers the question of individual liberty in an authoritarian regime of the early 1980s, just a few years before the fall of the Berlin Wall. Gerd Wiesler, the main character, is a devoted and loyal functionary of the socialist state. In fact, he has gained such a reputation as an interrogator that he conducts classes in the art of extracting information from the enemies of the state. And although some of his young students question the ethics of his methods, he maintains that any pain or discomfort suffered by the accused is solely for the purpose of extracting the truth. Moreover, in his private life we see a man who resides alone in a rather austere flat with little else in his life except his job. When he is given the task of investigating the main characters in the movie, playwright Georg Dreyman and his live-in girlfriend, actress Christa-Maria Sieland, he tackles the chore with his usual intense efficiency. He organizes his subordinates to set up a surveillance nest in the attic of the building where the suspects live, enabling him to hear and to see everything that occurs in their home.

But what he discovers is the reverse of what he has been led by his superiors to expect. It soon becomes clear that the playwright is not interested in overthrowing the state; rather he focuses for the most part on writing his plays. He is friendly with and loyal to those who are subversives but encourages them to develop their various talents and not to become obsessed with politics. Finally, Wiesler sees that the relationship between Georg and Christa-Maria is not a bohemian arrangement but involves deep and abiding love on both their parts. Soon discovering that the party official is forcing Christa-Maria to have an affair with him, Wiesler realizes that the suspicions concerning Georg are false, a trumped-up case on the part of the official to get rid of his rival for the affections of Christa-Maria.

But the turning point for Wiesler is a musical one. Upon hearing that his good friend and the former director of his plays who was blacklisted by the party has committed suicide, Georg plays the score given to him by his friend, entitled "Sonata for a Good Man." From this point onward, Wiesler's allegiance turns from his superiors to the two suspects being wrongly accused of crimes against the state. Why? Jameson's remarks on Beethoven and Hegel are particularly pertinent:

A satisfactory reading of Hegel's thought at any point resembles in structure the listening demanded by the Beethoven sonata, where the part, the note or phrase, must be apprehended both in itself and in respect to its position in the whole, as variation, reprise, modulation, and so forth (*Marxism and Form*, 47).

Listening to Georg playing, Wiesler feels the harmony of part and whole not only in the music but between Georg and his friend; artistic and personal integrity are joined. Now Wiesler refuses to be a party to corruption and, unlike his old school-friend, the Minister of Culture, he has no ambition to advance in the bureaucratic hierarchy, at least not if the price is being involved in a sham investigation. Wiesler's personal integrity provides the motive and the surveillance, the means to subvert the system. And it is notable that Georg's decision to turn on the government by publishing in the West an article on the suppressed high rate of suicides in the East is also prompted by a personal, not an ideological motive. Neither Wiesler nor Georg seem interested in undermining communism: they both wish to root out and remain apart from personal corruption. Georg and his girlfriend show Wiesler that art, be it music, drama, or acting, like individuals, has its own orbit, its own integrity, as an intrinsic part of the whole.

Wiesler discovers the personal integrity of Georg and Christa-Maria by analyzing their inner form, by entering into their world like an actor in a play. First, moved by the physical aspect of the love of Georg and Christa-Maria, he hires a prostitute in what appears to be a new experience for him. Second, he arranges for Georg to discover the affair between Christa-Maria and the party official, and he pretends to be a fan of hers in order to advise her to stop this arrangement. Finally and most importantly, he removes the incriminating evidence, the typewriter, from its hiding place so that the police will not find evidence against Georg. And at this point the musical motif of the "good man" reappears. When Wiesler tells Christa-Maria that she has enough talent to prevail without the help of the party official, she calls him a "good man." At the end of the film when Georg discovers from the archives that Wiesler was his savior, he writes a novel dedicated to Wiesler, entitled *A Sonata for a Good Man.*

Near the end of the movie one scene is devoted to the good man. Suspected by his superiors of helping Georg and Christa-Maria evade the authorities, Wiesler was demoted to a menial job in the Stasi mail room, and now, after the fall of communist East Germany, we see him delivering mail. In the window of a bookstore he sees a new novel by Georg, goes in, opens the book, sees the dedication, buys a copy, and when asked if he wants it gift-wrapped, replies, "No, it's for me." The good man is the one who refuses consciously to participate in corruption, for although he lies and withholds evidence he does so to protect those he knows to be innocent. He made a conscious choice and remains willing to abide by the consequences. The party official, on the other hand, has now become, or so it appears, a successful businessman who continues to torment the innocent, telling Georg that the police knew he was unable to satisfy Christa-Maria's sexual needs, something we know to be untrue.

Here we note that Wiesler's personal integrity has given him a place in a book, since his integrity shares with literature a kind of inner form. By

POST-MARXISM, FREDRIC JAMESON

contrast, the corrupt party official leads Georg to express his dismay that such people could ever be in charge of a country. Near the end of the film, after Georg has discovered that Wiesler saved him and sacrificed his career in the process, he takes a taxi to his address. On the way, seeing him delivering mail, he observes but does not approach him. In the next and final scene, over two years later, Wiesler discovers the book dedicated to him. We infer that Georg decided that the most appropriate form of gratitude would be a book dedicated to him that presumably tells the story we have seen in the film, or at least part of it. We never find out if the subject of the book is Albert Jerska, the director who committed suicide, or Wiesler, or both. In any event, both men are examples of those who sacrificed their careers to maintain personal integrity. One possible form of this narrative could be to show how an officer in the Stasi, an organization devoted to "knowing everything," comes to respect the right to privacy of the innocent, or the lives of others. We have moved one stage beyond "Il Postino." In the end, Mario, we recall, shares the spotlight with Neruda but is not the subject of Neruda's poetry. Georg's decision to write a book dedicated to and probably about Wiesler represents his desire to make a place for him in history, to provide for future generations an alternative to the Stasi file of a disgraced officer. By incorporating the novel, *A Sonata for a Good Man*, within the film, we are given an instance of how the individual has a place in history, an inner form, so to speak, within that of the film, a bold Hegelian assertion.

But a Marxist might wonder to what effect, how does Wiesler's story change the direction of history. In particular, the question is can we protect the good man, the man who refuses to follow orders to victimize the innocent even at the risk, like a "whistle-blower," of being himself victimized? For Jameson this problem is formulated in terms of the relationship between Hegel and Marx, that is, between the spirit of the individual and the apparatus of the state.

Hegel and Marx: "The Constant Gardener"

Jameson formulates this problem as follows:

> We will try to redefine the role Hegelianism is called upon to play in a Marxist framework: the problem is clearly at one with the relationship between the values of the older middle-class revolution and revolutionary consciousness and needs of the present day. Yet it is at once evident that the very principle at work in the dialectical analyses [...] that of the adequation of subject and object, and of the possibility of reconciliation of I and not I, of spirit and matter, or self and world—is itself

100   FILMSPEAK

the very premise of Hegel's system and may be claimed to be virtually Hegel's intellectual invention (*Marxism and Form*, 44).

As the title, "The Lives of Others," makes clear, the issue is not ideological. Wiesler does not reconsider his commitment to communism. Rather he expects the communist state to accommodate the lives of others, that is, to permit individual liberty that is lawful and does not infringe upon the freedom of others. Indeed, his training as an interrogator has been the acquisition of expertise in the art of making just such a distinction. Of course, the "vulgar" Marxist may assert that East German communism should not be judged on the basis of those who abuse its principles. But Jameson's inner form points to something different from judgment of the regime. His method suggests that no socialist state can abide in history without tolerance of Hegelian self-consciousness, an issue that is given prominence in "The Constant Gardener" (2005), directed by Fernando Meirelles, starring Ralph Fiennes as Justin Quayle and Rachel Weisz as his wife Tessa.

The film opens with Justin Quayle standing in and reading a lecture for his superior, Sir Bernard Pellegrin, Head of the Africa Desk at the British Foreign Office. The theme of the lecture is that the only viable alternative to war is diplomacy. The film goes on to show that some forms of diplomacy can be as lethal as war. At the film's conclusion, Pellegrin is publicly exposed as the source of the death of numerous Africans, many of whom are infants, in that he knew that a crime was being perpetrated and, instead of preventing or exposing it, tried to cover it up. But what are we to make of this conclusion? Will those who replace Sir Bernard and his confederates in crime be any less corrupt than their predecessors, particularly as those higher up in the Foreign Office may also be implicated in the crime but remain in place? Such, I believe, would be the traditional Marxist view. Jameson, however, encourages us to pursue the inner form, which leads to a different point.

The inner form involves the relationship between Quayle and Tessa. Quayle is a fine example of British diplomacy. Congenial, diffident, self-effacing, quietly intelligent, he serves the government to the best of his capacity but is aware of the limitations of what can be done in a deeply troubled society like that of many African nations. At one point, when he and the pregnant Tessa are riding in a car, she asks him to give a lift to an African family that needs to get to a nearby hospital. He replies that he has to put her health ahead of the local family's medical need. Thus Quayle attempts to maintain his personal integrity by protecting his family, his private life, while doing his best as a public official. He is a keen gardener, which for a well-educated diplomat would be associated with the end of Voltaire's *Candide*, where cultivating one's private garden is presented as an alternative to being disillusioned and manipulated by the social and political forces in the public world. Indeed Quayle often retreats to his garden when public matters become difficult, finding more genuine pleasure in horticultural pursuits than in his job.

Tessa, when we first see her, is a fearless young student who asks Quayle questions that he cannot answer and that embarrass the government he represents. But instead of being put off by her aggression, he admires her courage and forthrightness. Eventually they marry and go to Kenya, with the understanding that she will be able to pursue her research on pharmaceuticals unhampered while he goes about his duties at the commission. In Africa, Tessa continues to ruffle diplomatic feathers, but Quayle remains tolerant, loving, and admiring of her courage.

But when Tessa dies in suspicious circumstances, Quayle moves out of his garden and becomes less the genial, tactful functionary and more aggressive and Tessa-like. In one episode, when Quayle has to make a hasty departure from desert outlaws, he asks that one of the local children be included in the rescue, reminding us of the earlier incident when Tessa asked him to take a local family to a hospital. In that earlier incident, he pointed out to Tessa that the country was full of people needing his assistance. In the later episode Quayle argues, as Tessa had earlier, that helping one is better than helping none. We see that Quayle has not only moved out of his private shell, his garden, but also has come to see the value of the individual even in a country that shows little regard for such a value.

His new attitude results in his discovery that shortly before her death Tessa had given the British High Commissioner a report indicating that officials in the British Government were involved with a pharmaceutical company that was using Africans as guinea pigs for a tuberculosis vaccine that caused the death of many. Eventually, Quayle finds out that Sir Bernard Pellegrin ordered the elimination of Tessa. Quayle realizes that, in making this information public, he too will be eliminated. But he makes a conscious decision to do just that.

The development of Quayle as a character constitutes the inner form of "The Constant Gardener." The point being made is that the familiar distinction between public and private, between Quayle's duties at the commission and his garden, can no longer be maintained. Indeed we later realize that the pesticide that he uses in his garden has some of the deadly ingredients found in the tuberculosis vaccine. A post-Marxist interpretation of "A Constant Gardener" differs markedly from a traditional Marxist reading that would probably focus on the fact that capitalism encourages the ambitious to pursue their individual economic advantage, that is, fosters diplomats who do not rock the boat or endanger the pursuit of capital. But corruption of government officials is, as we have seen in "The Lives of Others," not limited to capitalism. The Jamesonian Marxist would, I believe, focus on a diplomat of integrity, like Quayle, who feels in the end that there is no point in continuing a way of life that indirectly contributed to the deaths of his wife and many African children. He comes to accept that the basic assumption that his private life and that of his wife would be kept separate from the public sphere was unfounded. The issue here involves more than economics, since Quayle has no capitalist ambitions. Jameson insists that post-Marxism move beyond the old obsession with economics:

> The all-informing flaw of vulgar Marxism as such, may be traced to a misconception of the so-called economic level itself: for to the degree that the economic schema [...] purports to furnish a continuous model of economic development over a long period, to that degree it is itself an ideal and indeed often an unconsciously idealistic construct (*Marxism and Form*, 375).

Jameson is suggesting here that, in insisting upon the predominance of the economic, the vulgar Marxist neglects other elements, which in "The Constant Gardener" involve the main male character. Although it is true that the pharmaceutical company's deadly experiment is supported by the British Government for economic reasons, Quayle's personal development involves something else. His investigation of the matter results in a shock to his system that recalls Jameson description in the following terms:

> A Hegelian criticism includes an essentially critical, negative, rectifying moment, one which enforces upon us an abrupt self-consciousness with regard to our own critical instruments and critical categories. When we turn now to a properly Marxist criticism, it will be through a similar epistemological shock that we will be able to identify its presence, for such a shock is constitutive of and inseparable from dialectical thinking, as the mark of an abrupt shift to a higher level of consciousness, to a larger context of being (*Marxism and Form*, 375).

Quayle is shocked to discover not only that his government is implicated in the corruption but that an entire network of people are involved in risking their lives to expose the corruption. And when near the end he faces his friend and superior, Sandy, head of the British High Commission in Kenya, with proof of Sandy's contribution to the death of Tessa, we see the effect of the shock of self-consciousness upon someone who had previously been driven by the economics of personal ambition. Hence Quayle's new self-consciousness has an effect not only upon Quayle and the audience of the film but also on one of the perpetrators of the crime. Moreover, Quayle goes on to sacrifice his life in order to expose Sir Bernard Pellegrin, the person who asserted at the beginning of the film that diplomacy achieves what violence cannot. Is not Quayle's letter to his brother-in-law exposing Pellegrin a final act of diplomacy, one that insists upon diplomacy based upon acceptance of personal responsibility? The inner form of "The Constant Gardener" encourages us to ask whether the individual of good conscience can alter the economic forces that impel civilizations to act in contradiction of their highest values. But of course the Marxist, old or new, will point out that, even if the conclusion of "The Constant Gardener" suggests the possibility of reforming the British position, what about the Africans themselves, equally implicit in this crime, whom, we recall, Tessa, had exposed at one of the embassy parties. A new question now arises: if the third world is a part of the problem and not the solution, what is the alternative, how are we to proceed to help the third world? To address this question, I turn to "Invictus," released in 2009, directed by Clint Eastwood and starring Morgan Freeman as Nelson Mandela and Matt Damon as François Pienaar.

Economics and history: "Invictus"

The title refers to the poem written in 1875 and published in 1888 by William Ernest Henley that concludes with the famous lines: "I am the master of my fate / I am the captain of my soul." Mandela explains that, when in prison on Robben Island for 26 years and at his lowest moments of despair, these lines inspired him to go on. Henley's assertion of self-reliance is clearly at loggerheads with the central Marxist assumption that all individuals are subject to social and political forces beyond their control. It is one thing to accept that Mandela used these lines for spiritual sustenance but quite another to believe that the reformation of South Africa after apartheid could be based upon such a principle. In the film, Mandela suggests that the Springbok rugby team adopt Henley's philosophy, thereby improving their chances in the World Cup and uniting a new South Africa. The vulgar Marxist focusing on outer form would be likely to see the film as a futile attempt to convince us that South Africa can be led out of isolation and back into the international community by individual grit and personal determination.

Once again, by pursuing inner form we may find a more viable and complex position. Very early on in the film, after being elected president, Mandela starts to institute a policy of reconciliation with the Afrikaners that is highly controversial and adamantly opposed by many of his party. On his first day as president, he invites the office holders who worked with the previous administration, almost all of whom are Afrikaners, to stay on and continue in their positions under his leadership. He is opposed in this policy by his own advisers and members of his family, but he persists. And we see a microcosm of the problem when Mandela assigns Afrikaners who under apartheid had been members of the secret police to join his personal bodyguards, bolstering the protective shield of the president. As the head bodyguard points out to Mandela, these are the people who tried to kill us. Mandela replies, that is in the past, but reconciliation with our enemies is necessary for the future of the country.

Not surprisingly, however, the relations between the Blacks and the Afrikaners are tense and fragile. So Mandela decides to use the Springbok rugby team to unite the country. Why? Because during the term of his imprisonment he saw the Afrikaner guards playing rugby while the Black prisoners played soccer. For this reason the opening scene of the movie, Mandela being driven from prison, shows the cavalcade passing the black ghetto with the children playing soccer on one side and, on the other side, the Afrikaners playing rugby. Indeed, so important is the sport of rugby to the Afrikaners that the members of Mandela's party vote to change the name of the national team, the Springboks, and their colors, both of which are associated by the blacks with their oppressors. Against the advice of his advisers, Mandela takes the risk of confronting these party members and narrowly convincing a slim majority of them to reverse their vote. His next move is to meet with the captain of the Springboks, to impress upon him the symbolic importance of the team. Lastly, we see that the Springboks have been ordered, "from the very top," to go into the black communities to teach the black children how to play rugby.

Mandela believes that the country needs a national sport and that this goal of reconciliation can only be achieved if the blacks avoid doing what their oppressors expect of them, imposing their sport on the white population. Of course, the winning of the World Cup was hardly something Mandela could have counted on; it was a wonderful added bonus. But the object was to get all the different colors of people to root for one team. And the point that is being made is not that politics is like a game of rugby. Rather that the only possible way for South Africa to move forward is by way of cooperation between the Afrikaners and the Blacks. Freedom from oppression requires more than release from prison; the individual can only realize his or her full potential if there is order in and proper management of the country. And the Afrikaners alone have the expertise for that. Certainly, history has borne out Mandela's judgment, particularly if Zimbabwe is seen as the alternative.

Furthermore, Mandela's goal is not individual freedom. A Marxist whose old followers address him as "comrade," he is keenly aware of the larger forces constricting the individual. In fact, he spends most of his presidency traveling to the richest first world nations to convince them to invest in South Africa. François Pienaar's father jokes at one point that perhaps soon Mandela will visit South Africa. The reconciliation between Blacks and Afrikaners serves a social, political and economic end: South Africa has the labor, management, and resources, the infrastructure, necessary to encourage foreign investment. While outer form might see here a naïve assertion of self-reliance, inner form shows a subtle approach to the global market.

The resistance that Mandela confronts from both his party and that of the opposition involves for Jameson an outmoded concept of class: instead of a class as a way "of relating to and refusing the others," post-Marxism suggests that "each class implies the being of all the others in its very being":

> Such a relational concept of class [...] will necessarily imply the shock of demystification in its very structure. It will always presuppose a movement from an apparently systematic, coherent, self-contained surface to that historical situation behind it in terms of which the ideological product under examination suddenly proves to have had a functional and strategic value as a weapon of a determinate kind in a concrete and local struggle (*Marxism and Form*, 380–1).

Mandela understands that reinforcing class division between Blacks and Afrikaners, the working and middle classes, will prove fatal to the entire society. So he chooses rugby as a means of "shock" in order to "demystify" the old ideological battle between these two classes, not to subvert the Marxist concept of class but to achieve a concrete goal, preserving the very fabric of the society. Why? Because, he recognizes that none of the rich nations will invest in South Africa if they believe it is not capable of managing its affairs. Again, his approach to global capitalism is not as a capitalist. When a secretary points out to Mandela that he has not collected his salary for months, he is shocked at how much he earns and decides to donate a third of it to charity. His approach to capitalism is similar to that of China, to enter the global economy without completely accepting the entrepreneurial ideology of the West. But while China invests, Mandela attracts capital that can be used for purposes suitable to the specific needs of his country. In that respect, Mandela's contribution is in bringing Marxism to bear upon the concrete struggle of South Africa, that is, upon history.

The last and most emphatic point to be made about Jameson's post-Marxist view is that, while his innovation involves inner form, he ultimately comes to outer form or to the place of the present, the local, whether literary or actual, in history. To return to Jauss's astronomical image, inner form is the orbit of a planet and outer form is the larger cosmological system of which the planet is a part. But while Mandela's great achievement in "Invictus" is to have brought about a sense of unity, at the end of the film it remains to be seen what will be achieved by this newly formed whole. And I expect most would agree that the answer to that question is still unfolding in history. A less vague sense of what Jameson means by history as the container of inner form is illustrated by a movie entitled "Made in Dagenham," directed by Nigel Cole, released in 2010, and starring

Sally Hawkins as Rita O'Grady, Miranda Richardson as Barbara Castle, Rosamund Pike as Lisa Hopkins, and Bob Hoskins as Albert Passingham, the union representative.

History as the container of inner form: "Made in Dagenham"

This film is an exercise in "faction" since it is based upon accurate historical facts concerning an episode that occurred in the UK in 1968, namely the strike by female machinists at the Ford factory in Dagenham on the outskirts of London. But it is not completely a documentary, because the leader of the strikers, Rita O'Grady, is a fictive creation—a composite figure made up of the historical characters involved—and the personal stories of the characters are not based on historical evidence.

But the point of the film is decidedly historical: that is, first to explain why, in 1970, two years after the strike, Great Britain passed a law requiring equal pay for women; and, second, to remind us that many other Western countries soon followed with similar legislation. In the next chapter I shall analyze this film in more detail in relation to feminism. Here my focus is the framing device or outer form; the film begins with information about the sewing machinists' strike of 1968 and concludes with reference to the Equal Pay Act of 1970. In this sense "Made in Dagenham" is a film about the relation between inner and outer form, between the quotidian lives of ordinary people and history. Jameson describes such a move as a shift involving historical distance, a point made emphatically in the film by the use of Mary Quant and Biba fashions, heavy cigarette smoking, and most importantly actual newsreel footage from 1968 reporting on the Dagenham machinists' strike. Jameson explains:

> Such a shift is essentially a function of historical distance itself, of the focus on historical events; from far away cultural objects seem to reflect their situation or infrastructure in a relatively passive way, and this is neither true nor false but the implication of the medium itself (*Marxism and Form*, 382).

From this distant historical perspective of factory life more than 40 years ago, it seems so obvious that equal pay for women is fair and necessary that we are led to wonder what was the reason for resistance. The obvious answer is money; as the union leaders point out, a raise in pay for the women will only be realized by lowering the pay of men. Otherwise, as the Ford representative maintains, the factory will have to make its cars elsewhere in order to realize a profit. Capitalist economics lie at the heart of the problem. But the solution entails something else, the camera changing from the distant historical view to a closer perspective, as Jameson puts it:

> As we move closer and closer to such phenomena [...] the individual actors begin to emerge and we begin to become oppressively aware of the unique existential situations in which each of their acts springs into being; in such a focus, close up, classes are no longer even visible (*Marxism and Form*, 382).

Three women from very different backgrounds come together to alter the situation of the working conditions of the women of their time and generations after them: Rita, a machinist who lives on a housing estate, Lisa, a university graduate and the wife of the manager of the Ford factory, and Barbara Castle, the most prominent female politician of her day. Together these three alter the course of history, but not because they form a class or are part of a political party. They each have different stories to tell, inner forms that will be pursued in the next chapter because they are feminist narratives. My point here is that the historical facts of 1968–70 concerning equal pay for women encompass—actually the relationship is dialectical—the inner form, a factional yet comical account of the daily lives of those involved on both sides of the strike. But, as Jameson reminds us, inner form is a hermeneutical problem, that is, one requiring interpretation, and that interpretation will explain the relation between inner and outer form. It should be clear at this point, however, that each of the three women achieved a new level of consciousness, a concept Jameson attributes to Hegel, in order to have an effect upon the realm of Marxist history. Jameson's innovation shows us that individual ethical acts, from the top, Nelson Mandela, to the middle, Justin Quayle, or to the bottom, Mario the postman, Gerd Wiesler, and Rita O'Grady, can be significant in Marxian terms, a notion that traditional Marxists would dismiss as "bourgeois propaganda."

Having now completed the analysis of five male theorists in this and the previous four chapters, I turn to the work of Hélène Cixous, who provides a female alternative, but not one that completely subverts those of her male counterparts.

CHAPTER SIX

Post-feminism: Hélène Cixous

Summary: *The chapter begins by explaining that Cixous was chosen because in addition to her critical works her creative writings are an integral part of her influential feminist position. The main innovative element of Cixous's theory is procedural, an aspect influenced by Derrida, but one which reaches an ethical resolution. The first axiom of Cixous's theory, "writing with the body," is explained by way of "Julie and Julia." While the female body may serve as a form of communication, the next section, on "Made in Dagenham," explains how feminism affects human behavior. The source of this power to change how people act is the libido, which is illustrated by "Marie Antoinette." The female libido is to be distinguished for Cixous from its male counterpart, as is seen in the analysis of "Moulin Rouge." In the next section, "Rosenstrasse" illustrates how the female libido alters the male power structure. But this type of change may be only temporary: "The Devil Wears Prada" shows how women can make a permanent change within the establishment. The conclusion distinguishes Cixous's process from that of Derrida by its emphasis on care, affection, and love, all functions of the libido, that produce ethical results not only in larger social and political terms but also for individual love relationships.*

The decision to choose one feminist is difficult because the United States, Great Britain, France, and other countries are marked by distinct types of feminism, to say nothing of the individual differences within each country.

But I have chosen Hélène Cixous because, as a Joyce scholar as well as a novelist and playwright, she is one of the most influential critics in the field and, unlike many feminists, both her critical and her creative work bear directly upon literary theory. Cixous deconstructs the very notion of literary theory while articulating an alternative theory: the manner in which she avoids what she calls the "male master theory" while positing her own theory can best be understood by proceeding through this chapter, that is, by following her procedure. The very fact that this view can only be understood by following it in process is crucial, for the alternative, an all-encompassing concept, would be another example of male mastery.

Writing with the body: "Julie and Julia"

Cixous believes that poetry has direct access to the unconscious where the repressed, that is to say, women, "manage to survive." The antidote to female repression, according to Cixous, is to write: "Write yourself. Your body must be heard. Only then will the immense resources of the unconscious spring forth. Our naphtha will spread throughout all the world, without dollars—black or gold—non-assessed values that will change the rules of the old game" ("The Laugh," 879). But female writing is of a special sort:

> [...] women must write through their bodies, they must invent the impregnable language that will wreck partitions, classes, and rhetorics, regulations and codes, they must, submerge, cut through, get beyond the ultimate reserve-discourse, including the one that laughs at the very idea of announcing the word "silence," the one that, aiming for the impossible, stops short before the word "impossible" and writes it as "the end" ("The Laugh," 881).

A film that may help us understand the notion of writing through the body, "Julie and Julia," was written and directed by Nora Ephron, first released in 2009 and starring Meryl Streep as Julia Child and Amy Adams as Julie Powell. The element of the body is most evident in the fine portrayal of Julia Child whose physical presence, so imposing on her television cooking show, is vividly conveyed by Meryl Streep. From the 1960s I recall a tall, gangly, somewhat disjointed, jolly woman with a high-pitched voice often giggling at herself for messing up her own recipes, a trait that endeared her to America's young cooks. Her cookbooks contained the sort of detail that beginners or, in her terms, "cooks without servants," required, particularly young Americans being exposed for the first time to the complexities of French cuisine. In short, Julia Child's cookbooks seemed to anticipate her own errors in the kitchen, mishaps that later became television spectacles. The most characteristic of these is Julia's attempt to flip an omelet that ends up with only half of it in the frying pan. In that sense she was writing her own body. In an account of her early life, Cixous tells of her awkwardness as a woman contemplating entry into the male world of writing:

> So for the Sons of the Book: research, the desert, inexhaustible space, encouraging, discouraging the march straight ahead. For the daughters of the housewife straying into the forest. Deceived, disappointed, but brimming with curiosity. Instead of the great enigmatic duel with the Sphinx, the dangerous questioning addressed to the body of the Wolf: What is the body for? Myths end up having our hides. Logos opens its great maw, and swallows us whole (*Portable Cixous*, 46).

In the film, Julia is a sort of "housewife straying into the forest" when, unable to decide what to do with her leisure time, she enrolls in a French cooking school. Meryl Streep portrays a gawky American woman among the subtle, delicate French all-male would-be chefs. Somehow she bumbles her way through the classes, endearing herself to some of her classmates by her self-deprecating humor and enthusiasm. A few of her French female friends ask Julia to help them write a French cookbook in English, and it is by way of a version of this cookbook that we come to the character of Julie.

Julie is also writing her own body and is a "housewife straying into the forest," but now we are transported from the Paris of 1949 to twenty-first-century New York where Julie's writing takes the form of a journal on a computer for her blog. Recently married, Julie is bored with her job and seeks solace in cooking. She decides to devote a year to trying every recipe in Julia Child's book (524 in all), and to record the results on her blog. The portion of the film devoted to Julie Powell is a visual version of her blog writing, an expression of a young woman's withdrawal from public careerism in the Big Apple to a private nest of family and home cooking.

While, as Julie points out, she and Julia resemble one another in that both were bored secretaries who turned to cooking for pleasure and relief and, we might add, struggled to find a mode of communicating their experience, a book for one and a blog for the other, their home lives are different. Paul, Julia's husband, is unfailingly supportive of Julia, and they live a comfortable upper-middle-class life. Julie and her husband struggle to make ends meet, and because she must continue working at least part of the time, her cooking often results in neglect of her husband who, on one occasion, leaves her for a few days. Nevertheless, in the deepest sense both husbands support their wives, and that love and support are seen as crucial to their success, that is, getting into print and becoming a successful blogger. The women in the film are therefore at a post-feminist stage where the wife's career need not exclude her traditional role in the family. But neither Julia nor Julie is a feminist in any overt sense; they are struggling to write about a traditionally female endeavor, cooking, in a male-dominated publishing world. Not surprisingly, both women are discovered by females, Julia by an editor and Julie by a reviewer. Cixous explains the reason:

> In women's speech, as in their writing, that element which never stops resonating, which once we have been permeated by it, profoundly and imperceptibly touched by it, retains the power of moving us—that element is the song: first music from the first voice of love which is alive in every woman. Why this privileged relationship with the voice? Because no woman stockpiles as many defenses for countering the drives as does a man. [...] There is always within her at least a little of that good mother's milk. She writes in white ink ("The Laugh," 878).

It is important to realize that Cixous is not asserting that feminine writing is somehow exclusive to women. Indeed, some men are more capable of it than some women, but they are the exceptions rather than the rule. The distinction between male and female writing is cultural, not natural. The passage above was first translated into English in 1975, and the cultural situation has undoubtedly changed somewhat, but perhaps not drastically. Writing nearly 20 years later, Cixous formulates the issue in different terms:

> If someone were to ask me, [...] if I would like to have/be a man's body to try it out, I would say "of course". I would be fascinated to know the world from another body, to be able to really work on sexual difference from one side and from the other. [...] But I will never pass over to the other side no matter how good the approximation is (*Portable Cixous*, 56–7).

Sexual difference is not wholly confined to gender but can never be completely bridged. This complex paradox is explained by Cixous in an anecdote about her personal experience:

> I spoke as if the characters in this scene were: a woman, and a man, obviously. Such a scene with such characters is no doubt possible, there could be a man who is a man-without-any-doubt, a woman who is a woman-without-any-doubt. But I know from experience (I only know anything after experience, that is, after errors) that very often a "woman" is not a woman, nor a "man" a man. [...] I know a woman who is at second glance an ensemble of five little boys and one little girl (*Portable Cixous*, 57).

Since gender differences persist, Julia Child's cookbook from the middle of the last century has a special resonance for Julie Powell as a woman in the present. Again Cixous explains why: "There always remains in woman that force which produces/is produced by the other—in particular, the other woman. *In* her, matrix, cradler, herself giver as her mother and child; she is her own sister-daughter" ("The Laugh," 880).

But although Julia inspires Julie, an inspiration that initiates Julie's journal and results in her book (and the film), Julie is crushed to discover, near the end of the movie, that Julia was not favorably impressed by Julie's work. It is not clear why this is so. Julie murmurs something about lack of respect that is never further pursued or explained. This personal problem is not of interest because the more important point, as Julie's husband points out, is that the image Julie has of Julia is what matters; in a sense the virtual Julia is more significant than the "real" Julia. What Julie comes to accept at the end is that Julia is now a figure of discourse, an image produced by her writings, her television spectacle, and the writing as well as the presentations about her. So the movie ends with Julie's husband photographing her at the Smithsonian exhibit honoring Julia Child. The place where women share their femininity or feminism is in the realm of discourse, and that is why Cixous encourages women to write their bodies. But the object of this writing is not merely to set up personal relationships between women, for, as we have seen, Julia is not interested in a friendship with Julie. Yet the movie demonstrates that there is a clear discursive relationship between the work of these women, and that Julie's success is a direct result of the writing of Julia. Cixous's feminist realm of discourse is not impeded by personal animosities. Yet the result of this discursive relationship is, for Cixous, distinctly feminine.

The way we do something completely differently, the way we passionately love the same person—Language—differently: this too can be seen by reading our texts.
  I will evoke various positions of the body-in-writing. For me, in the beginning, there is nothing. I begin without words and with body. It is a letting myself go to the bottom, letting myself sink to the bottom, a collecting together of the soul. Let us wait. This requires an unconscious, an unformulated belief in a force, in a materiality that will come, that will manifest itself, an underground sea, a current that is always there, that will rise and carry me (*Portable Cixous*, 59).

The important connection between Julia and Julie is discursive, between Julia's cookbook and Julie's blog, the two different forms of discourse accounted for by differences of personality and of historical era. The film adds a dimension to this discourse by demonstrating that Julia and Julie are both blessed with husbands who love them deeply. Indeed, as Julie asserts, echoing the exact words of Julia, she could not have succeeded without the devotion of her husband. The love that pervades these two marriages is present in both the background and the foreground, the encouragement of the husbands and in the women's works, their books and blogs. For it is the love communicated by the book, the blog, and indeed the film that speaks to the audience of these forms of discourse, that inspires women (and men) of Julia's and Julie's generation.

The goal of feminine communication: "Made in Dagenham"

The next question that arises is that while women writing their own bodies may encourage others to join in the discourse, as seen in the influence of Julia's book upon Julie, what, apart from personal development, is the goal of this process? And here, I believe, is Cixous's major innovation. The goal is not to imitate "male mastery"; rather, she wishes to deconstruct this concept. Deconstruction is a major influence upon Cixous. In fact, for 35 years before his death in 2004, Derrida encouraged, read, and shared conferences and books with Cixous. She has written two books on Derrida and made clear how important his position is to her in the following terms: "Deconstruction will have been the greatest critical warning gesture of our time" (*Cixous Reader*, xvi). Nevertheless, as we shall see, Cixous clearly distinguishes herself from Derrida.

> It is impossible to *define* a feminine practice of writing, and this is an impossibility that will remain, for the practice can never be theorized, enclosed, coded—which doesn't mean it doesn't exist. But it will always surpass the discourse that regulates the phallocentric system; it does and will take place in areas other than those subordinated to philosophico-theoretical domination. It will be conceived of only by subjects who are breakers of automatisms, by peripheral figures that no authority can ever subjugate (*Portable Cixous*, 35).

To understand this challenging innovation, a theory against traditional theory, we may examine in greater detail the film that was briefly discussed in Chapter Five, "Made in Dagenham." In the previous discussion, this film served to illustrate the manner in which the beginning and end, namely, the information about the strike of 1968 and the Equal Pay Act of 1970, literally and figuratively enclosed the factional middle of the film, giving it historical significance. The Equal Pay Act is also of theoretical significance, for it introduces a new idea into the global economic market, that gender should not be a factor in determining salary.

And yet the female sewing machinists had only a more local goal in mind. Equal pay for Dagenham, yes, and perhaps with luck equal pay throughout Great Britain, but never in their wildest dreams throughout the Western world. So how did it happen, how did the local and practical become general and theoretical? To answer this question we turn to the middle of the movie, the progress of the strike. Rita soon realizes with the help of Bob, the union representative, that the first and most important obstacle in the women's way is the male workers at the Dagenham factory. As the union leaders point out to her, any raise in pay for the women will be realized by giving less to the men. Similarly at home, the women who lead the strike soon experience resistance from their husbands who have to fill in for their wives, that is, attend to the children and other household duties that were not previously their responsibility.

Rita courageously faces both of these challenges by deconstructing male mastery. She confronts her husband and the male union leaders head on, and in that sense she uses male aggression against males. But she speaks with her body and thereby evokes love in her husband and admiration in the union leaders. One episode illustrates both tactics. When summoned to the office of the Secretary of State, Rita pays a visit to Lisa, the wife of the general manager of Ford Dagenham. When he answers the door she is less flustered than he, asks for his wife, and later emerges in one of Lisa's dresses. Here we see Rita's versatility, firm posture with the husband, gentle solidarity with wife—"I need a favor." Interestingly, the relationship between Rita and Lisa began when both decided to confront a male teacher whom they believed was bullying their children. Lisa organizes a petition against this teacher, asks Rita to sign, and tells her later that they have won. The teacher has been asked to leave the school.

Emboldened by this victory, Lisa goes to Rita's home, encouraging her to continue with her strike against her own husband. Why? Lisa explains that, although she is a graduate with a first-class degree from an excellent university, she is treated by her husband like a fool, or in Cixous's terms, a "stray housewife in the forest." The communication between Rita and Lisa is not textual but involves speech and body language:

> The woman-body, for me, is the place *from where*, the soft place from where girls or boys, humans, descendants are born, this place "below the belt" which is like two hands, like tomorrow, and has more than one memory, a memory of what has taken place, a memory of what will take place (*Portable Cixous*, 57).

Their resulting friendship means that Rita, wearing Lisa's Biba dress—bolstered by the male-like comradeship and the female-like fashionableness—feels confident enough to confront and negotiate with the government official.

Most importantly, she adopts a similar double strategy with Barbara Castle, the Secretary of State, a mixture of male straightforwardness and female solidarity so that Mrs Castle, instead of being put off by Rita's effrontery, is emboldened to use the same tactics with Prime Minister Harold Wilson. And the reason this tactic works is because Rita never hates or excludes men. Cixous explains as follows:

> Besides, isn't it evident that the penis gets around in my texts, that I give it a place and appeal? Of course I do. I want all. I want all of me with all of him. Why should I deprive myself of a part of us? I want all of us. Woman of course has a desire for a "loving desire" and not a jealous one. But not because she is gelded; not because she's deprived and needs to be filled out, like some wounded person who wants to console herself or seek vengeance. I don't want a penis to decorate my body with. But I do desire the other for the other, whole and entire, male or female; because living means wanting everything that is, everything that lives, and wanting it alive. Castration? Let others toy with it. What's a desire originating from a lack? A pretty meager desire ("The Laugh," 885).

Rita changes from the dutiful wife who works at the factory into a leader, first of the women and then of both the men and the women. And yet she never leaves her previous self behind; she remains a devoted wife and mother even if her new responsibilities necessitate some neglect of her domestic duties. Cixous explains that women can change without deserting their past and how that inner personal development shapes their public persona. To understand this notion I shall examine Sofia Coppola's "Marie Antoinette," released in 2006, starring Kirsten Dunst.

Deep down inside: "Marie Antoinette"

"Marie Antoinette" begins with a 14-year-old heroine arriving from Austria to become the wife of the Dauphin, the future king of France. She is not at all experienced in matters sexual or political and is completely unfamiliar with the ways of the French court. But even at the outset we begin to see distinctive elements of her personality. She refuses to abide by many French conventions, insisting on accompanying her husband when hunting, and snubbing the King's mistress, Madame du Barry. Cixous explains that women soon see through the inanity of "propriety":

> I say women today overturn the "personal," for if by means of laws, lies, blackmail, and marriage, her right to herself has been extorted at the same time as her name, she has been able, through the very movement of moral alienation, to see more closely the inanity of "propriety,"

the reductive stinginess of the masculine-conjugal subjective economy, which she doubly resists ("The Laugh," 883).

The early scenes after her arrival at Versailles are full of inane forms of "propriety." We see a naked young woman shivering as decisions are made and then revised as to who is at the top of the hierarchy of dressers. Marie Antoinette is remarkably patient but clearly amused at the arbitrary, farcical element of the ceremony. Similarly, the ritual surrounding the royal couple eating breakfast, repeated until the palace is sacked during the revolution, becomes a sort of chorus. Facing the courtiers, they are served from behind—itself an elaborately conventionalized performance—eating in the presence of but not speaking to a standing audience. The film is punctuated by empty ritual. The other notable example of inane propriety concerns Madame du Barry, who is insulted that Marie Antoinette has not spoken to her, since the rule of court is that she may not speak until spoken to by the princess. Out of consideration for the King, Marie Antoinette, who despises the woman, speaks briefly to her, occasioning an approving nod from the King. All in all, a scene worthy of a farce.

Once settled in, Marie Antoinette begins to enjoy the extravagant pleasures of the court. But soon she is under great pressure to produce a male heir and eventually restricts herself to a small retinue, retiring to the Petit Trianon that becomes her own private court. Although lavish, this setting is considerably less extravagant than the King's court. She then moves on to Le Hameau, which in its own highly romantic, idealized way is simplicity itself, at least in comparison to the life at the main Château de Versailles. Here we begin to see the Princess maturing, recognizing the limitations of the court and the courtiers. We also learn that the famous phrase attributed to her, "let them eat cake," is inaccurate and taken out of context. Life inside and outside of the court is having its effect upon the young princess.

On the one hand she has constituted herself necessarily as that person capable of losing a part of herself without losing integrity. But secretly, silently, deep down inside, she grows and multiplies, for, on the other hand, she knows far more about living and about the relation between the economy of the drives and management of the ego than any man. Unlike man, who holds so dearly to his title and his titles, his pouches of value, his cap, crown, and everything connected with his head, women couldn't care less about the fear of decapitation (or castration), adventuring, without a masculine temerity, into anonymity, which she can merge with, without annihilating herself because she is a giver ("The Laugh," 883).

Near the end of the film, as the revolution approaches, we see the full development of Marie Antoinette's personality. She has now produced two male heirs, one of whom dies in early childhood. Those close to the King and Queen advise them to leave Paris or risk their lives and those of their family. But although deeply protective of her children, the Queen repeatedly asserts that her place is to remain beside her husband while sending her followers and advisers to the country. When the mob finally arrives, her first thought is to protect the children. And in leaving Versailles she and the King display a quiet dignity that we have not seen in them before. The film ends before their death. Instead of showing their attempted escape and subsequent capture, we see the ruins of Versailles, suggesting that the personal development of Marie Antoinette, like the ruins of Versailles, is one of the neglected shards of history. The greatest change in Marie Antoinette is produced by motherhood, for in the end she is protecting not only her children and her retinue but also the King. Cixous explains this kind of motherly behavior as follows:

> In women there is always more or less of the mother who makes everything alright, who nourishes, and who stands up against separation, a force that will not be put off and will knock the wind out of codes (*Portable Cixous*, 34).

The personal development of Marie Antoinette from a naïve Austrian aristocrat into a Queen and a mother makes her execution for using her privileged position at court to evade responsibility as Queen as farcical as the inane conventions at Versailles. But the film is designed to show us that what happens to this young woman during her time at Versailles is a distinctly feminine kind of inner growth that most males cannot understand because it is radically different in kind from that of men. Consider, for example, the moment when Marie Antoinette appears on the balcony before the mob and bows her head, reducing them to silence, moved by something they cannot comprehend. Sofia Coppola shows us that this historical moment of coming into womanhood has been neglected by historians, and Cixous explains that such female historical moments are neglected because they involve the female libido:

> We will rethink womankind beginning with every form and every period of her body. [...] Because the "economy" of her drives is prodigious, she cannot fail in seizing the occasion to speak to transform directly and indirectly all systems of exchange based on masculine thrift. Her libido will produce far more radical effects of political and social change than some might like to think (*Portable Cixous*, 34).

We recall that the libido became an issue in this film when a courtier was obliged to make clear to the young King how one goes about making babies, a key factor in the process of maturation of both the King and the

Queen. Indeed only after sexual congress has been completed do the King and Queen form a bond that permits them to respect and influence one another. Prior to that moment, their relationship was purely conventional, another hollow ritual. But a far more detailed examination of the function of libido in the social and political fabric of life is seen in "Moulin Rouge," released in 2001, directed, produced and co-written by Baz Luhrmann and starring Nicole Kidman as Satine.

Female libido: "Moulin Rouge"

Another illustration of Cixous's conception of the personal development of the female can be seen in the film "Moulin Rouge." Again, the conclusion of the movie highlights the change in the heroine. It will be recalled that Satine is the courtesan/opera star who wishes to be an actress. She believes that the Duke, the sponsor of the opera, will support her ambition if she satisfies his desires. But she falls in love with Christian, the poet/songwriter, who has no money and cannot therefore advance her career. Zidler, the director of the opera, encourages Satine to please the Duke so that he will continue to sponsor the show.

In the final climactic episode of the movie, when the opera is being performed, Christian is in despair, knowing that Satine has agreed to spend the night with the Duke. But in spite of the fact that Satine knows her career will be ruined, she decides, upon seeing Christian from the window of the Duke's apartment, not to betray her beloved. Why is she drawn to the poet? Because "the poets," Cixous insists, differ from the novelists in not being "allies of representationalism. Because poetry involves gaining strength through the unconscious and because the unconscious, that other limitless country, is the place where the repressed manages to survive: women, or as Hoffmann would say, fairies" ("The Laugh," 884). Cixous's point is made in the movie by way of music, since the songs are themselves a kind of poetry, and the genre of the musical prepares us for a dénouement indicating that the star of the show will turn out not to be a common prostitute. Music mediates between the realm of economic reality and that of the "fairies." Cixous explains why the "fairies" are important to women:

> Yes I realize that in talking of a fairy, I am a bit less afraid. I sense that with the help of a fairy I can say and do whatever comes, and above all whatever I believe and thus think without worrying that what "I think", as soon as it is said, will instantly be annihilated by a great blow of reason, of my reason, not necessarily his reason, or denial (*Portable Cixous*, 48).

But although the fairies help women express themselves, the problem remains how do they communicate with men, the source of power, who dwell in the land of reason. In the film this problem arises when the Duke threatens to stop the music, the cinematic equivalent of the land of the fairies. The Duke insists that the end be changed so that the poet/painter does not win the heroine. And so, in the end, the drama of the rivalry between the Duke and Christian intrudes into the opera itself. The Duke sends an assassin after Christian, but the actors on stage prevent him from shooting Christian, and then the Duke himself tries to kill him, only to be prevented by Zidler, the opera director, because "the show must go on." Nothing can stop the deep human desire for the world of poetic imagining and love. Christian wins Satine, but then she dies in his arms, finally succumbing to the consumption that we have known about but that has been kept a secret from the two rivals

The conclusion of the film is complex. Satine and Christian win in that the conclusion they want for the opera is realized. Nevertheless, Satine's death prevents the resolution they wished for themselves. But death, as Cixous warns us, is always a part of the power of the female libido. Satine breaks through the economic, rational power of the Duke in the form of discourse, not reality. Those viewing the opera doubtless believe that her death is a part of the show. Thus the opera, poetic music, communicates the power of the female libido in that Satine has prevailed against the Duke, keeping the end in which the poet/musician wins the heroine. And since the audience response is wild applause, the Duke may keep his investment in the show since it appears to be a moneymaker. Thus economics remains in control, the pressure of which undoubtedly contributed to the death of Satine. How, we are left to wonder, can feminine libido affect the nature of the power structure, change the establishment, particularly if male economic forces remain in place?

One important step toward this end is achieved in "Moulin Rouge" when the opera within an opera creates a tragic heroine out of a courtesan. The traditional moral hierarchy is deconstructed by way of female libido; the first step in changing the male power structure is altering how men think. The idea of Cixous that is here manifested can be better understood by considering how her creative work relates to her critical position. Early in her career, Cixous reevaluated the Oedipus myth. "The Name of Oedipus" is a tragedy about the love of Jocasta and Oedipus. Clearly, the incest taboo that of course seals their fate has little effect upon the intensity of their love:

Jocasta Life opens up, it is within me, it is before me, it expands. And it is us. A breeze ruffles my hair. It is the breath of life.

Oedipus Why? Why? Why are you woman? How are you woman? You must give me the whole of her everything.

(Portable Cixous, 230)

Unlike Sophocles' version in which the marriage of Jocasta and Oedipus is taken to be a political alliance between the former Queen and the new King, here we have a passionate love match with no moral regrets, no mention of incest or the deception of the gods. Rather the tragedy concerns the demise of the female libido and, appropriately, Jocasta only wishes that love could protect them:

Jocasta I was absolutely sure. This morning a burning wind wakes me.

My bed goes up in flames
Time! Time has caught fire.
Leaping toward you my blood is ablaze.
I dash—
The ground gives way; love does not protect us.

(Portable Cixous, 235)

Jocasta's fiery love breaks through the incest taboo; her passion consumes Oedipus, altering his inner being, the way he sees the world. To understand how this process actually changes the world we turn to "Rosenstrasse" and a comic drama by Cixous.

Changing the world: "Rosenstrasse"

Released in 2003, "Rosenstrasse" was directed by Margarethe von Trotta, and starred Maria Schrader and Katja Riemann. "Rosenstrasse" is a story within a story. In the beginning Ruth Weinstein is mourning the death of her husband in New York City. Although the family is not particularly orthodox, Ruth decides to sit Shiva, a Jewish ritual in which the family and close friends sit on cushions on the floor, cover all mirrors, do not shave, answer the phone, or carry out their usual tasks for 30 days. During this period, the fiancé of Hannah, Ruth's daughter, arrives from South America to join in the mourning, but Ruth orders him to leave because he is not Jewish. At the end of the film we return to this New York apartment where Hannah and her fiancé are married and receive the blessing of her mother.

The story within the story concerns Hannah's trip to Berlin to find out about the past of her mother, since she refuses to talk about her youth during World War II. Hannah discovers that when Ruth, aged eight, was deprived by the Nazis of her mother, the last surviving member of her family, a Christian woman named Lena, took her home and looked after her for three years until the war ended. Pretending to be a journalist, Hannah finds this woman in Berlin and hears her story about the war, which is the story-within-the-story of the film. What becomes clear from this inner tale is that the Jew–gentile dichotomy that seems now to have such a hold on Ruth is a mask for an entirely different problem. Having lost her mother, Ruth becomes deeply attached to Lena, her German "Aryan" protectress, but then feels betrayed by this second mother when, after the war, she is sent to her aunt in the United States. Ruth believed that as a Jewess she was abandoned by her Christian mother. Hannah, however, discovers that Lena only let Ruth go because she thought it was better for the child. Indeed, Lena deliberately refrained from expressing her deep regret at the loss of Ruth in order to make the break easier for the child. In fact, Lena has always cherished some of Ruth's childhood keepsakes; Hannah returns to New York with a ring from Lena, which was to bring whatever a child wished. To thank her daughter for rediscovering and reinterpreting her past, Ruth gives the ring to Hannah. At the wedding that follows, Ruth welcomes her Christian son-in-law into the family with the same blessing that we have already witnessed in the inner story; when Lena's Jewish fiancé announced to his parents his plan to marry her, his mother kissed Lena uttering the same words. The framing device thus raises a serious question. How was a bridge formed between some Jews and some Christians in Germany during the period of rabid, systematic anti-semitism, probably the worst in all history and certainly the worst ever experienced in Germany?

To answer this question I turn to the inner story. Cixous's parody of "Hamlet" may help prepare us for this part of the film. Entitled "The Blindfolded Fiancée or Amelait," the scene here selected concerns the relationship between Gertrude (here called Gerutha) and Hamlet (Amelait). As the comical names suggest, the focus is not a consideration of Hamlet and the Oedipus complex or of Gertrude's implication in the plot against the elder Hamlet. Instead, Cixous focuses upon the quotidian life of mother and son. The *donnée* of this particular scene is that the "blindfolded fiancée," Reguine, the Ophelia counterpart, maintains some relationship with Amelait.

Amelait Will you come to our wedding?
Gerutha Where? When? It's gone this far and you haven't said a thing to me?
Amelait All right, then. We won't talk about it any more. I said nothing.
Gerutha Is this another joke?
Amelait And your wedding: Where? When? We could have a double wedding, a canopy for four. That's an idea, it would save some money. What do you think?
Gerutha These jokes in bad taste—ever since puberty.
Amelait Everything is tangled up, what's good tastes bad, tragedy is hilarious, death is holding its sides. Give me some more of the paté. You didn't poison it, I hope? Because I want to give her some.
(Portable Cixous, 273)

The comic/tragic parody of this scene involves an important concept for Cixous. In the midst of tragedy that, as we know, intimately affects both Hamlet and Gertrude, we have a mundane comic moment, sharing a cup of tea. In spite of deep-seated differences between them, differences that will shortly result in the death of both, they show us, by virtue of Cixous's deft touch, a certain wary affection, a bond between mother and son that we would expect to see at any family table. Differences, yes, deep differences. But differences that touch upon one another. Libido has always been the issue with Hamlet and Gertrude, but here it takes the form of ordinary family affection/connection. I want to suggest that it is precisely this sort of family relationship that changes history in the inner story of "Rosenstrasse." The problem here is that a group of "Aryan" wives have discovered that their Jewish husbands are being kept in a building on Rosenstrasse, and it is important to keep in mind that this part of the film documents an historical occurrence.

The women begin by trying individually to bring about the release of their husbands, speaking to Nazi officers and arguing that Jews married to Aryans are not to be treated as Jews. Having failed in their attempts to free their men by way of the bureaucracy, the women resort to more traditional female tactics. One wife begs for help from her aristocratic father who has disinherited her for marrying a Jew, but he refuses. Then she tries sex, spending a night in bed with an officer whom she hopes will effect her husband's release. That also fails. Gradually the women learn that traditional female wiles are futile, and so they end up together outside the building where their husbands are held captive. The first indication of the female solidarity that eventually ensues is the ruse the women use to find out if their husbands are inside, since no information about them has been given to the wives. One wife explains to Lena that she told the guard her husband had her house key: the reply the guard conveys from her husband indicates that he is alive and in the building. Lena then uses the same ruse with regard to her ration card to confirm the presence of her husband.

Here two key events occur. First, when it appears that their men are about to be deported to concentration camps they accuse the guards of being "murderers." Second, when a squad of machine-gunners is sent in to disperse or mow down the women with bullets, they stand their ground, simply looking directly at the gunners. In both instances, the women have replied to male aggression with neither aggression nor passivity. First they accuse the men of being less than men, namely murderers, killers of those who have done nothing to them. Second, they refuse to back down, almost daring the soldiers to harm or kill Aryan women very like their own wives. And this strategy miraculously wins the release of their husbands. Cixous explains this female kind of tactics:

Nor is the point to appropriate "men's" instruments, their concepts, their places, or to begrudge them their position of mastery. Just because there is a risk of identification doesn't mean that we will succumb. Let's leave it to the warriors, to masculine obsession with how to dominate the way things work—knowing "how it works" to "make it work." For us the point is not to take possession, in order to internalize or manipulate, but rather to dash through and to "fly" ("The Laugh," 882).

The women offer no resistance; nor do they threaten the men. The tactics of mastery are abandoned. They manage to oppose without suggesting that the men are to be displaced or in any way to lose their power, a male obsession. They fly above the battlefield. And flying, for Cixous, is a female characteristic: "Flying is woman's gesture. Flying in language and making it fly. We have all learned the art of flying and its numerous techniques; for centuries we have been able to possess anything only by flying. We've lived in flight, stealing away, finding, when desired, narrow passageways, hidden crossovers" ("The Laugh," 882).

In this instance the narrow passageway seems to be the firm but not shrill reminder by the women that they are no different from the soldiers' wives, mothers, and sisters. Male mastery is thus deconstructed. And the underlying drive that enabled these women to endure the cold nights waiting, to stand up to the German soldiers, and to outwit the guards is family affection, that same bond we saw between Amelait and Gerutha, and that here led Lena to adopt Ruth. And the power that resulted in the release of the Jewish husbands—a historical fact, as the film makes plain—is also the force that changes Ruth's way of thinking. Instead of a young Jewess being abandoned by an Aryan second mother, she is deeply loved and sorely missed by Lena. Thus, the film suggests that female libido affects history by changing how people think; we are left to assume that the Nazis released the men because they ceased to think of them as Jews but as husbands of Aryans.

Nonetheless, at the end of this film we are left to wonder whether or not these Jewish husbands were eventually transported. Although it is now generally assumed that these men did survive the war, it is not clear in the film whether they were merely given a temporary reprieve or did actually survive. Perhaps the filmmakers wished to reproduce the situation at the time when none of the wives or husbands would have known what were the Nazis' future plans for them. But even if the respite were only momentary, that would not detract from the achievement of the women. After all, to prevent one person being in a concentration camp for a single day was more than millions of people could achieve. In any event, the Nazi power structure was clearly only momentarily affected by these courageous women. How, we now must ask, can the female libido effect a permanent change?

Female difference and change:
"The Devil Wears Prada"

Released in 2006 and directed by David Frankel, "The Devil Wears Prada" stars Meryl Streep as Miranda Priestly and Anne Hathaway as Andy Sachs. This film demonstrates that when women become a part of the power structure, female alternatives are created. In "The Devil Wears Prada," Miranda Priestly is as devoted to her job and career as any man, and is undoubtedly a tougher and more demanding boss than most men. Not surprisingly, she pays a price in her family life, spending little time with her children and eventually being divorced by her husband. Yet she demands that her new assistant follow in her footsteps, which, again predictably, results in Andy Sachs alienating her partner. But in the end Andy chooses not to follow the career pattern of Miranda. She turns back to her partner and applies for a job that does not require a total life commitment. Surprisingly, Miranda does not hate her or try to ruin her career. On the contrary, she gives Andy a good reference and, in her final restrained nod, shows her understanding of Andy's decision, the very opposite of Miranda's choice for herself and of what she wanted for Andy. In short, Miranda had the power to stifle Andy's career, but decided to help rather than hurt her. Cixous encourages the female tolerance of difference:

We are pieced back to the string which leads back [...] Break out of the circle; don't remain within the psychoanalytic closure. Take a look round. Then cut through. And if we are legion, it is because the war of liberation has only as yet made a tiny breakthrough. But women are thronging to it. I've seen them, those who will be neither dupe nor domestic, those who will not fear the risk of being a woman, who will not fear any risk, any desire, any space still unexploited in themselves, among themselves or others or anywhere else. They do not fetishize, they do not deny, they do not hate. They observe, they approach, they try to see the other woman, the child, the lover—not to strengthen their own narcissism or verify the solidity or weakness of the master, but to make love better, to invent ("The Laugh," 885).

The end of "The Devil Wears Prada" suggests that Miranda's success as fashion editor, well beyond that of most men in the profession, is her recognition that her business is based upon free choice, women preferring her brand or style. And choice is only really present when there is the possibility to select another brand, or, in the case of Andy Sachs, another kind of career. Meryl Streep's brilliant portrayal of Miranda shows that her distinctly feminine power is in the ability to give up power willingly, another kind of deconstruction of mastery. Cixous describes this kind of female power as follows:

> Wherever she loves all the old concepts of management are left behind. At the end of a more or less conscious computation, she finds not her sum but her differences. I am for you what you want me to be at the moment you look at me in a way you've never seen me before: at every instant. When I write, it's everything that we don't know we can be that is written out of me, without exclusions, without stipulation, and everything we will be calls us to the unflagging, intoxicating, unappeasable search for love. In one another we will never be lacking ("The Laugh," 886).

Miranda teaches Andy by way of tough love. First, she tells Andy in no uncertain terms that her attempt to avoid fashion by dressing down is a form of self-deception. She explains that the "cerulean" sweater that Andy probably bought at a discount store for a song was originally created by her company at a high cost and with intense creativity. Eventually, Andy comes to understand that high fashion affects all women and that she is foolish not to take advantage of her position to listen to the fashion experts around her who show her how to dress to her best advantage.

The second lesson Miranda teaches Andy is the cutthroat nature of their world. When she promotes Andy to Emily's position, she insists that Andy tell Emily, that is, take responsibility for her decision to accept the position, to replace her colleague. Andy begins now to feel that this world is not where she wants to be, and here she teaches her boss a lesson. When the two are in Paris together, Miranda, moved that Andy tried to warn her about the possible loss of her job, lets her hair down for a rare moment. Acknowledging Andy's loyalty, she says that Andy reminds her of herself when younger and suggests that she has a great future in the business. When Andy replies that she is not sure that is what she wants, Miranda exclaims that everybody wants what the two of them have. Shortly thereafter, Andy quits, and to her surprise her new boss tells her what Miranda said in her reference letter: although Andy was a great disappointment to her, he would be a fool not to hire her.

Without compromising her high standards and her authority, Miranda has accepted Andy's decision to pursue another career. She has learned to accept difference, something that will serve her well as a mother. Female power, Cixous asserts, does not necessitate conformity. The devil who wears Prada is a different kind of boss from her male counterpart. Her acceptance of difference not only serves those who work with her but also makes her product more attractive to her customers, that is, appealing to their choice. In that sense, Miranda has altered the kind of person who can prevail at the top of the power structure. But Miranda comes by this ability,

Cixous implies, because she is a woman and maintains an element of her femininity in a male environment. How are men to learn to act in a similar fashion? How can a male come to understand that there is an alternative kind of power that involves giving power up, giving power to others?

The learning process of female love: "The Social Network"

A recent movie that suggests how men can learn from female love is "The Social Network" (2010), directed by David Fincher and starring Jesse Eisenberg. The plot is framed by Mark Zuckerberg, the founder of Facebook, failing miserably in an attempt to establish a relationship with a woman. In the first scene, Erica, his about to be ex-girlfriend, tells Mark that he is an "asshole," and in the final scene the young female lawyer exits with the line "You are not an asshole. You just are trying very hard to be." After both rebuffs, Mark turns to his computer, in the first instance posting insults against Erica, and later, after the lawyer turns down his invitation to a meal, gazing wistfully at Erica's entry on Facebook.

The body of the film, between these two scenes of failure with women, is about Mark's success, his male mastery in the big-money computer world. This realm is dominated by men; women, if present at all, are secondary, decorative ornaments or trophies. Yet Mark points out that the original goal of Facebook is to find a sexual partner. At the end of the film, the inventor of Facebook with his 25 billion dollars is alone at his computer. The loveless world of male mastery is sad and lonely. And we understand the distinction made by the woman at the end between an asshole and one trying to be an asshole as particularly apt for Mark. To succeed in his project Mark has betrayed his best friend and alienated the women in the film who seem to care about him. Yet it is clear that the real driving force behind Facebook is neither money nor prestige but frustration at his inability to find love. All the men in the film exploit women for sex and play the entrepreneurial system for money. Mark's best friend and financial officer, Eduardo, although more suave with women, has a disastrous relationship with his girlfriend. Instead of the "cool" world of the computer aspect of Facebook, Eduardo wants to master the financial world of big money through advertising. The final crisis with his girlfriend is appropriately an episode when she burns a present he has bought to placate her.

But while Eduardo finds his girlfriend's behavior incomprehensible, Mark is equally ill at ease in his "cool" world. He longs for female otherness but goes after it by way of male mastery. The movie leaves us with the view that Facebook is aptly named, a mere façade, virtual reality as a poor substitute for reality. At its best, Facebook serves as a means of moving beyond the computer to people, but Mark has imprisoned himself in virtual reality. Yet the end of the film is quite poignant. The young lawyer's final remark is paradoxical. If he is not an asshole, only trying to be one, the implication is that he could, if he wished, try to be something else. But that change involves a process, not simply a concept to be mastered, one that perhaps involves the rest of Mark's life. If so, it will have been initiated by a female who cared enough to suggest it to him as a possibility.

Cixous demonstrates that, in giving up our investment in male mastery and seeking an alternative, we gain a richer life, not only as theoreticians who can evolve beyond a single all-encompassing conception, but also as individuals, male and female, living in a world of individual differences, enjoying and profiting from difference. Cixous raises the notion of individual tolerance above the specific and local—the personal break-through—to the level of general principle or theory. The well-known Talmudic doctrine is perhaps applicable here: "He (or she) who saves one person saves the whole world." For Cixous, saving the other enriches us, our world, our being, thinking and living, theory and existence. But unlike any male master plot, any all-encompassing conception, tolerance of difference is a never-ending process with an ultimate goal that is unattainable.

Cixous formulates the way women confront male mastery as follows:

The relationship to pleasure and the law, the individual's response to this strange, antagonistic relationship indicates, whether we are men or women, different paths through life. It is not anatomical sex that determines anything here. [...] It happens culturally that women have more of a chance of gaining access to pleasure, because of the cultural and political division of the sexes, which is based on sexual difference, the way society has used the body and on the fact that it is much easier to inflict on men than on women the horror of the inside. After all women do all virtually or in fact have an experience of the inside, an experience of the capacity for other, an experience of non-negative change brought about by the other, of positive receptivity (*Cixous Reader*, 135).

To conclude, "The Social Network" provides a clear illustration of the difference between Cixous and Derrida, both of whom focus upon process. Derrida's method is tactical; he studiously avoids specific end goals. Cixous, however, is more goal-oriented. That is why she gives more emphasis to the libido, a drive that by its very nature is goal directed. Facebook is designed to help Harvard geeks find a sexual partner; all of Mark's accomplishments, including his fortune, are not for him sufficient consolation for the lack of a girlfriend. He is driven by libido. That is the source of the irony of the film and of its hope. As the young woman at the end points out to him, he is trying to be something that is self-defeating, that is, the kind of person no woman will want. The only hope, and it is a vague one, is that he may recognize the need to change his goal. Erica, the young woman at "BU" at the beginning of the film, provides the key for Mark. Near the end he tries to speak to her, but she refuses because instead of apologizing he tries to take up where he left off, and she understandably wants none of it. But the point that Cixous makes clear is that the libido, the sexual appetite, is always goal-directed, and in that regard woman has a special role to play, not merely to deconstruct men and their master narratives, but also to socialize them, helping them to be self-doubting compatible human beings. Wouldn't that be an improvement for Mark? Wouldn't that be an example of "non-negative change brought about by the other, of positive receptivity"?

"A conclusion in which nothing is concluded"

This title is from that of the last chapter of Samuel Johnson's *Rasselas* (1759), which was the subject of my first book some years ago. The goals of that book and this one are not markedly different. My interest has remained the ethical nature of interpretation. Ethics is usually defined as the pursuit of the "good life." The heart of ethics for me derives from the Talmudic principle previously cited: "He (or she) who saves one person saves the whole world." Interpretation is related to this notion because it involves hearing in the deepest sense the other; literature, like all the arts, is an expression of another. But the conversation that ensues between the interpretive reader and the text must be goal-directed, that is, we need to attend, not to what we want to hear, but to what the other is "getting at," the writer's purpose. By this means literary interpretation is related to life; we are much less likely to save someone, in the ethical terms of the Talmud, if we do not listen to him or her. This principle is most prominent in our lives in the field of medicine. Having carefully and perceptively examined the patient and read the text, usually in the form of test results, the skillful doctor pieces together the subjective and the objective to arrive at a diagnosis. The art of medical interpretation is an ethical act involving reading and personal interchange, and although we do not think of literary interpretation as involving matters of life and death, one could argue that in the great tragedies, particularly *King Lear*, just such matters are at stake. I have written a number of books about this interpretive process: those interested in the details of my view should consult the bibliography. My point here is to confess that every analysis of a theory or a film in this study undoubtedly bears the stamp of my predilection for ethical interpretation. Instead of once again advancing that view, risking a form of what Cixous calls male mastery, I think it would be more useful to reflect on the question of why literary theory relates to commercially successful movies. In this respect, I am following Johnson's example. *Rasselas* is a story about the quest for the "choice of life"—the modern rough equivalent would be a career choice—but, as the title of its last chapter suggests, no resolution to that question is found. The implication at the end of that narrative, as I read it, is that one should eliminate choices of life that impede the quest, mindless or mind-numbing careers, because Johnson believes that knowledge, seeking to learn about choices of life, makes us less unhappy than remaining in complacent security. I wish to leave the choice of a master-theory quest, a conception that envelops all of the others, open to the reader, with the suggestion that to avoid theory altogether is to lessen our understanding and enjoyment of life.

Movies of the past 25 years relate to theory because these ideas enrich the art of cinema, that is, help to sell seats and stimulate thought, giving pleasure and also nourishing the mind. Why? Theorists are subversives, not necessarily in the political sense, but in that they articulate innovative ideas that question established assumptions. For that reason, all the theorists analyzed in this volume use deconstruction, a strategy, as we have seen, for unraveling the seams of accepted truths. But they are not revolutionaries; their writing is far too complex and difficult to be directed at what the postman in "Il Postino" calls "*il popolo*," the people. Their interest is in the articulation of new ideas, which are directed at their colleagues in specialized fields of study. Even when these ideas seep into general discourse, they are clearly understood by few and only vaguely familiar to many. The term "deconstruction" is in common parlance, but it is seldom used in a way related to the formulation by Derrida. Woody Allen's "Deconstructing Harry," the single instance in this study of a movie-maker showing familiarity with a term of literary theory, uses deconstruction in a way that requires little knowledge of Derrida's writing. And, as you will recall, I found deconstruction more pertinent to Allen's "Everyone Says I Love You" than to "Deconstructing Harry."

My point is not that theory is somehow embedded in modern movies; rather, theory helps us understand how the film-makers achieve their ends and movies help explain theory. When Tarantino portrays a Nazi who can understand what it is to be a Jew without ceasing to be a Nazi, deconstruction is vividly exemplified and enables us to understand this character. Illustrating Foucault's concept of "power-knowledge," Slumdog learns the answers to the quiz questions by understanding the power structures that control the slum. "A Single Man" shows us simultaneously the situation of the homosexual in the 1960s and in the present day, thereby clarifying the reader response conception of "horizons of expectation." "The Reader" poses a problem about the unconscious as language that Lacan helps resolve: how can a seemingly decent woman live with her Nazi past for 15 years and only after learning to read accept responsibility. "Il Postino" raises a Marxist question about the relationship between the public and the private domains. Jameson's concept of inner form makes clear how the postman's love for Beatrice is related to the larger political forces that result in his death. And finally, Cixous helps us understand how Rita, in "Made in Dagenham," can bring about the reform of women's rights without threatening men. Rita thus serves as a fine example of Cixous's feminism. The interesting innovations of theory aid our understanding of what is new and entertaining in films that vividly exemplify the theoretical ideas: the interaction between film and theory works in both directions, each throwing light on the other.

Nevertheless, the chasm between theory and film remains. (Have I deconstructed myself?) The writings of the theorists are, to use Boswell's phrase for a Johnson poem, "as hard as Greek." Cixous refers to them as the "incorruptibles" because they make no concession to the common reader. By definition, the films included in this volume are accessible to a broad audience, but corruption, as we all know, is rife in the film world. The problem is that the popular arts need to attract audiences by suggesting innovation, but do not always fulfill their promise. John Dryden anticipated this problem in his satirical poem, "MacFlecknoe" (1678). The title refers to Dryden's contemporary, Thomas Shadwell, who was a very successful comic playwright. At the time, comedies were as popular as movies are today. Dryden takes Shadwell to task for tempting audiences with new ideas but then concluding his plays in the same old ways. Dryden explains that Shadwell can make more money by leaving new and disturbing ideas unresolved, "never deviating into sense." Audiences leave the theater complacently applauding the status quo. The result is new wine in old bottles or, as my students put it, a "Hollywood cop-out."

Some of the films analyzed in this volume may well fall into this category. But, as is pointed out in the Introduction, my object has been to show how theory is clarified by film and film is clarified by theory, not to judge the artistic merit of the films. Experts in the field of cinema criticism may well advance a justified critique of them like Dryden's of Shadwell. Nevertheless, film and theory share a search for innovation, whether that be mere appearance or the real thing.

The fact that literary theory pertains to a wide range of films, as is indicated by the list of "Films Analyzed," suggests that some theories which when first formulated in the 1970s and 1980s were considered erudite and obscure have in the more recent decades become part of the "Zeitgeist," the spirit of the age. My students have taught me, as was pointed out in the Introduction, how these ideas have now become a part of their "horizons of expectation." Our conversations with our children and grandchildren will rest in part upon understanding the rudiments of literary theory.

"The King's Speech," analyzed in Chapter Four, received four Academy Awards, for Best Picture, Best Actor, Best Director, and Best Original Screenplay. How do we explain the commercial success and professional recognition of a film about a king with a speech impediment? The interest in George VI as a historical figure and the wonderful acting, directing, and writing are not sufficient to explain this phenomenon. Surely the ideas in this movie must play a part in its success. We have already considered the Lacanian notion that personality is a function of finding a place in discourse, finding our voice. But now, since the film has gained what one Hollywood newspaper called "a royal flush," it relates to every idea in this book.

"The King's Speech" deconstructs history. The reign of King George VI is seen as a man's struggle with a stutter without in the least detracting from the King's personal dignity or historical significance. And mastery of the stutter is never wholly achieved, which is in part what makes him so endearing to and respected by us. We see the vulnerable element of the monarch, the seams of power that remain to the end present if less obtrusive. As Bertie experiences power-knowledge in coping with an overbearing father and a brother who cruelly mimics his stammer, Colin Firth finds himself as the star of a low-budget British film that has stormed Hollywood. Bertie is seen as a sensitive and loving father doted on by his children, and Firth announces at the Academy Award ceremony with the witty self-effacement worthy of Bertie that he fears his career has peaked.

The appeal of the movie and the actor pertains to reader-response. George VI is catapulted to fame as the "people's King," the royal leader of Great Britain during World War II, and Colin Firth achieves equal status in the theatrical world for his ability to excel in both comic and serious roles in part because his theatrical technique combines both sad laughter and serious smiles. An element of the ordinary person, of ourselves, is always there. Even post-Marxism has relevance here. David defeats Goliath; Hollywood bows to the little guy. Why? Because they admire the inner form and structure of the movie, how the actors, actresses, writers, and set designers have together molded a cohesive and beautiful whole, a moving spectacle without sex or violence. Lastly, Firth's great talent points to feminist ideas. The previous year he won the same award for playing a homosexual in "A Single Man." Doubtless part of Firth's talent is that male mastery and female flight are both manifested in his performance. As Helena Bonham Carter, herself nominated for an Academy Award for her part in the film, remarked when asked if she were disappointed not to have received the award, "But my king won." Surely, these ideas from literary theory must have contributed to the artistic recognition and success of this film. Literary theory is becoming part of the fabric of our culture.

The final question that usually arises is how do these six different theories fit together? I prefer to leave them with their differences. Perhaps some overarching concept could be provided that would include them all rather like a large leaky tent, but I wonder how useful a structure it would be. Fredric Jameson is very persuasive on this point:

> Theory emerging after the end of great philosophical systems, in a kind of market environment, has tended to become a whole set of different name brands. If that seems too frivolous to say, then we can say that

theory exists as named theories, as specific idiolects or private languages. The whole point of the philosophical system is to take a mass of ideas in the air of all kinds and give them a single coherent language, conceptuality, and set of terms. In that sense, the end of philosophy means that no one thinks that coherence is possible any more. This means that we have to speak all these theoretical languages all at the same time. There really is no way to synthesize them into a master language; nor is there even a desire to do so (*Jameson Reader*, 150–1).

Perhaps we now live in an age of eclecticism in which we combine various theories or languages, as Jameson calls them, to resolve concrete problems. Philosophy, that is, one all-encompassing theory, may be the last absolute to pass out of history. We cling to it, just as we do to the belief that democracy is the best system for all peoples of the world, with less and less conviction. If so, I hope for a responsible or ethical eclecticism, one that is dedicated to understanding the different theories, to combining them in ways that are not completely contradictory and inconsistent.

Suggestions for teaching literary theory by way of movies

Introduction

The first step in teaching literary theory is getting the students to engage with the material. Most are at first put off, believing that it is all beyond them. So I organize the course with the requirement that each student does an oral report on one theorist and two on a film. Given at the beginning of class for a maximum of five minutes, these reports are designed to begin discussion. The point is not that the student reporting is supposed to master or teach the theorist. Instead, he or she should raise questions, pointing to passages that troubled or interested him or her. My strategy here is to engage the entire class in discussion: I make clear at the outset that if you do not participate when someone else is giving a report you cannot expect that person to come to your aid when you are reporting, They are all in it together, and the result is that they understand a good deal more than they believe they do. For the instructor, the function of this initial discussion among the students for a maximum of 20 minutes is that you discover what for them are the problems and the issues. I divide up the week into, say, three classes with the first on the theorist and the following two on one film each. In a 15-week term considering six theorists, you then have two weeks for each theorist. Each two-week period involves two sessions on theory and four classes on films.

The films present a different problem. The students see them as mere entertainment and tend to judge rather than analyze them. I emphasize that the point is not whether you like them or not, or whether you believe they are good or bad. Rather, the object is to interpret them as you would a work of literature. Some try to apply the film to the theory, but I discourage that. My preference is that they analyze the movie in itself and leave the application to theory to me. The main difficulty is convincing them that commercially successful movies can be worthy of interpretation. With regard to viewing the films, I have found that most educational institutions have a central computer that links to all of the student computers. All the films of the class can be copied into this mainframe, with a password to protect copyright, so that the students may watch the films whenever they wish. Obviously, you do not have enough time to show them in class, and trying to arrange for showing them outside of class inevitably involves for some students conflicts with their other classes or extracurricular activities.

Once the reports and student discussions—again, 20 minutes—are concluded, I then begin by asking questions, particularly of those who have not spoken earlier. Given that the films are available online and that theory assignments are no more than 30 pages in length, there can be no excuse for not being prepared in class. And I would emphasize that the assignments are to be completed before class begins, and that the students will be expected to participate, having done the reading or seen the film. I restrict my comments to the last 15–20 minutes, trying to formulate a position that relates to and incorporates points made by the students in discussion.

The requirements for the course are three oral reports, two papers, one short and one long, and a final exam. The short paper is due during the fourth week of term and involves a three-to-five-page analysis of one theory essay to be taken up in class after the papers are handed back to the students. I have a conference with each student about the short paper and plan with them an individual topic for the long paper, which is due during the 12th week of term. The long paper involves a work of art, literature, film, or any plastic art that is of particular interest for them. Their assignment is to find in the library two critical essays that apply two different theories to this work and to assess the utility of these essays toward better understanding of the work of art. The object here is to emphasize the practical utility of theory and the ability to use more than one theory, since most of the students will find some use from both theories. The ultimate goal of the paper is to show them that theory proceeds generically, that is, by combining and modifying past theories. The final exam uses a question that the students raise during the semester: can the films that have been applied to one theory be applied to another? Yes indeed, and that is what I ask them to write about on the final, namely, to analyze two films to illustrate theories other than those that these films were used to exemplify in class. Some teachers are shameless.

Chapter One: Deconstruction

Derrida is in many ways the most difficult of the theorists included in this volume. My students have found his writings often frustrating and hard to follow. As an introduction, I suggest that the students watch the documentary film about Derrida, entitled "Derrida," (2002), directed by Kirby Dick and Amy Ziering Kofman, starring Jacques Derrida and

Marguerite Derrida. This movie gives a human face to Derrida and includes enough biographical information to satisfy their curiosity for historical detail. Although of little help in understanding Derrida's ideas, the movie does make clear what are the important insights and how Derrida is to be distinguished from the philosophical tradition in which he was schooled.

With regard to reading assignments, I would suggest short pieces, two or three of no more than 20 pages each. To prepare the students for the reading I stress that no one finds them easy, and encourage the students to read for the gist of the exercise and not to stop because they do not understand a specific term or allusion. It is helpful to explain to students before they read the material what are the concepts you are interested in pursuing but without dictating the outcome of the discussion that will follow.

I devote one class a week to the writings and two a week to exemplary films. You may prefer to study them together. However you organize the course, I would stress that the students approach the movies in their own terms quite apart from theory: what do you like or dislike about the film, what do you think is its point or artistic goal? Many students are eager to anticipate how you will use the movies to illustrate a theory. I tell them to leave that chore to me. I need the work. The students are, in my experience, more likely to become engaged with the issues if they analyze the films as films in their own terms. Then you can move on the interpretive level from the films to theory; moreover, you will thus be able to make clear that the bridge between film and theory requires moving beyond description and thematics to interpretation. For this reason, I would suggest that my chapters be assigned after your discussion or lecture. In this way, the students will come to understand that the agenda for consideration of these theorists is not fixed, whether by me or anyone else. Also, this procedure can result in analysis that may well lead to questioning my interpretations of the films and the positions of the theorists.

With regard to Derrida in particular, I would give a brief introduction to two or at most three ideas: for me, the choice would be on decentering and originary myths, but many other possibilities could be chosen, such as "différance" and "trace." It is also a good idea to point to particular passages in the readings that will be the focus of analysis in class and to stress that student reports should pay special attention to them. Finally, if the class has less than 30 students I warn them that each will be asked to speak about the assignment, even if only to explain what they do not understand and where they first became lost. The function of this exercise is to show them that they are neither alone nor particularly dense, and that their fellow students and most teachers had the same problems. Once you show them that the problem passages are not random but shared by most of us, you have located focal points for discussion and analysis.

As I suggested in the Introduction, the biggest obstacle in the beginning is convincing introductory students that theory is not merely for some higher order of beings who speak in a language no one else understands. Rather, it is about the sort of problems we confront in reading texts, literary or theoretical, and the concepts that help us resolve these problems. Of course, this conception of theory is based upon the premise, considered in the Introduction, that theory is not a branch of philosophy but devoted to solving the problems of practical criticism at a higher level of generality.

Giving the students a working understanding of the concepts in the reading assignment is very important. To explain decentering and originary myths I have on occasion asked students to provide examples from their other classes where practical criticism of texts has led to questioning unexamined assumptions. Alternatively, I use current events. During the recent banking crisis, I pointed out that one of the most conservative presidents of the United States had nationalized American banks, a position beyond that of those on the far left, let alone the right. Thus a binarism between left and right is decentered and an originary myth, the nationalizing of free enterprises as a strictly Marxist decision, is understood to be a myth.

Once the students begin to understand that deconstruction is a procedure that can be applied to any human creation, particularly literature and ideas, they will grasp how other theorists use deconstruction to call into question established positions and to find the "seams" for innovation, As Derrida says near the end of the film "Derrida," he would like to hear about the elements of the lives of philosophers that they avoid, such as their sex lives, because that leads to fissures in their thoughts, new possibilities for theory.

I stress during the sessions devoted to the theorist's writing that a vague understanding of the key ideas is sufficient. During the sessions devoted to the films, student conceptions will sharpen as they have specific examples to help ground their insights. Remind the students you are not suggesting that the writers and movie-makers have any more familiarity with theory than they do: the connection between the films and theory is a pedagogical and interpretative move on your part, not a historical or biographical statement.

I use no more than two or three movies for each theorist, depending on the size of the class. Most students are much more at ease with the movies than with the written work, but I have always encountered resistance when urging them to the interpretive level with films. Many assume that commercially successful movies are written solely for that purpose and that the search for some higher artistic purpose is futile. In some sense that serves your goal, since it enables you to stress that you are the source of the interpretation that relates the film to, in this instance, Derrida. But you may want to warn them that the entire issue of interpretation and what it entails will be a topic taken up by the hermeneuticists in Chapter Three. At this stage I stress two points: 1) interpretation serves the purpose of this class, using movies to illustrate ideas. All interpretations have a purpose or goal;

2) interpretation is dedicated to understanding the goals of others, in this instance, the film-makers. By this means, I hope the "use" of films is to be distinguished from "exploitation," that is, disregard of the intrinsic artistic purpose of the film in its own right.

Finally, I have found that the entire question of what constitutes interpretation as opposed to historical description or thematics is the subtext of the course. Most of my students had been trained by formalists who had no interest in theory. Historical descriptions or themes were ends in themselves. I found myself constantly driving the students beyond these insights, asking why see the movie, why read the book. In short, a prerequisite to understanding the use of theory is defining the nature of interpretation. Theory can then be seen to address the problems of interpretation.

Chapter Two: Michel Foucault and "power-knowledge"

I begin the discussion of Foucault with a consideration of the notion of discourse, since it is the basis of what for me are his two most important insights, "author-function" and "power-knowledge." Discourse should be understood as every form of communication, from the grunts and groans of breakfast companions to billboards and text messages, from graffiti to novels, from train whistles to symphonies, from porn magazines to museum pictures. We are unaware of this element of our life because we are immersed in it: we swim in it every day. Moreover we change strokes habitually, that is, alter our discourse with each new situation. Our conversation, for instance, in the classroom is very different from that among friends at a party. The different ways of speaking have to do with what Foucault calls disciplines: we are so imbued with the rules and conventions of disciplines that we forget that violations of them involve punishment. If you tell your professor as opposed to your roommate that you did not do the reading assignment because you preferred to go skiing you will be punished in terms of your grade.

"Author-function" is the result of the disciplines of discourse. To continue with the above example, you may say to your professor that you are sorry that you could not complete the assignment but would welcome the opportunity to make it up. Now, without telling a lie, you have moved deftly into your "student-function" which is much more likely to minimize a penalty. An author who achieves the stature of "author-function" need not lose personal integrity or have an "identity crisis." He or she, like any decent swimmer, one familiar with the conventions of the medium or discourse, responds to the currents and waves, the powers beyond individual control. We all respond to these kinds of forces so regularly in our daily existence that we are only subliminally aware of them. Full awareness results in what Foucault calls "power-knowledge."

The concept of "power-knowledge" involves not only power as the force of discipline in discourse but one other crucial factor, the limiting of knowledge, Foucault's major insight. To continue with the example of the student and professor, suppose the student after making up the assignment offers an interpretation and, when asked for evidence of his or her opinion, replies, "That is my interpretation and it needs no further justification. All of our views are subjective and everyone has a right to their opinion." The student will again be punished with a low grade, even though his or her opinion may, if properly documented, be intelligent and innovative. By violating the rules of the discipline of the discourse, here of literary criticism, the student's views are dismissed, not considered as false or incorrect, but as not within the realm of knowledge, not "within the true," not admitted to the club, fraternity or sorority of knowledge. And, I stress, the greatest and most innovative ideas often question the rules of the discipline, the power of "power-knowledge," as is the case with Foucault himself and all the other theorists in this volume. Derrida, for instance, is still dismissed by some philosophers as someone not writing philosophy.

The implications of this insight are vast and various. Once the students grasp it—and where is "power-knowledge" more manifest than for students?—they will start to go everywhere with it. The films provide useful perimeters of control because at first students associate the notion of "power-knowledge" with dogmatism and what I call "tyrant-teachers." But the films show that "author-function" and "power-knowledge" apply in situations apart from these abuses of pedagogy. They apply to free thinkers who wish to impart or permit freedom of thought to others. That is why Foucault asserted near the end of his life that he had devoted himself, not to a study of power, but to ethics, how people could help themselves as well as others to negotiate with power to achieve self-expression. At this point I send the students off to watch the films with this advice: have a genuine conversation with the films. Cinema is a form of self-expression; try to see that your interpretation comes to terms with what you believe to be the point of the film.

Once we get to the films, the task is much easier because the students naturally identify with the main characters who are all, in one way or another, students in that they are placed in environments where survival or achievement of their goals requires learning. The concepts of discourse and discipline are all defined in terms of what the protagonists wish to achieve. And that achievement is marked by an ethical end that is distinguished from "foil figures" whose achievements are corrupt, like that of Lord Wessex versus Shakespeare, Salim as opposed to Jamal, David and Jenny, the Black Swan and the White Swan, and Daniel and Mark. Proper self-expression for Foucault is always ethical, for it involves not only negotiating with power but also acquiring knowledge that helps others achieve the same end and opens the discourse to new kinds and forms of selfhood.

To explain Foucault's concept of the ethics of the self, I use the example of the dance, overtly present in "Black Swan" and the conclusion of "Slumdog Millionaire" but implicit in the other films. Nina finally experiences self-fulfillment when she becomes for a moment the black swan, and at the end Slumdog and Latika dance on the station platform in celebration of their love. The discipline involved in Nina's dance is painfully obvious, but Slumdog and Latika are carefully choreographed and must dance in unison with the others, a sort of equivalent of the corps de ballet. These three people achieve self-expression by dancing with others and never, literally or figuratively, treading on the toes of the other dancers. The self becomes manifest as part of a social network, which constricts its movement but permits individuation to be realized in the world, that is, to be seen and heard by others. In that sense, the self is forwarded by forwarding the selfhood of others. And for Foucault such a procedure promotes new kinds of selfhood: Latika is a prostitute, an outcast of society, and then she is a bride celebrating her marriage in public on the railway platform.

Chapter Three: Reception theory: Wolfgang Iser

It is usually helpful to explain that Iser and Jauss were colleagues at the University of Constanz in Germany and that this theory is derived from the German metaphysical tradition of Kant and Hegel, to mention only the two most important sources. Students enjoy reception theory because it is less abstract then the previous two theories and opens up new possibilities for them. But it is a theory vulnerable to two abuses: 1) anything goes, all interpretations are of equal value; 2) the end result is awareness of the premises of interpretation, a form of self consciousness. With regard to the first, it needs to be emphasized that the text limits interpretation and that the gaps and blanks are created by the work of art and not solely by the responder. Reading, in the deepest sense, attending to the otherness of a work of art and, by extension, to another person, is at the heart of this theory. In fact when students ask why does Iser limit himself to literature and not generalize about art, I answer that literature is the most exacting form of artistic otherness; misreadings can be empirically demonstrated. Also, reductive readings, non-interpretive or minimally interpretive readings are immediately apparent. Literature overtly demands careful attention to the text and yet requires that we go beyond the text, or fill in the gaps, by way of interpretation.

With regard to the second problem, self-conscious navel-gazing, I emphasize that such a view was present in the early stages of reception theory and that is why most of my citations are from the later work of Iser, from the 1980s onward, when he began to develop his notion of criticism as a form of anthropology. Self-reflective criticism becomes much more fruitful and interesting when applied in a cultural context, and that of course is where Jauss's concept of "horizons of expectation" comes to the fore, where we see the interplay between the cultural assumptions of our time and those of the age of the work of art.

At this point I find that most of my students are fascinated by history but know little about it. It is therefore worth making clear that most historians now accept that historical writing is a mixture of past and present. Almost no one now believes that history is a social science, capable of objectivity. Hence, Jauss's model for historical criticism is a model of history itself. Both have a built-in ethical dimension, namely, the reasons for choosing or selecting what is important: for the critic, what horizons are important and why.

Now you confront the problem of teleology: attending to the final goals of art and of the students' attempts to explain art. As we all know, most students are not pushed to their full potential. I, therefore, find that in-class analysis of the final goals of their papers is helpful. For they seldom go far enough, and it is easy to push them further by asking, or better yet, encouraging the other students to ask, "So what, why should I care?", an exercise that shows them they are not getting to the telos or final goal, whether theirs or that of the work of art. But with some exasperation at my insistent "so what" questions, they can get there and discover that description only becomes interpretation when it arrives at intentionality.

Any of the films will serve well for this exercise. Why does the "The Da Vinci Code" end with the double V in the Pei pyramid? Because God is not limited to one gender, good students respond. So what? Why should we care whether or not God is a male chauvinist? Because the alternative is to burden women with more original sin than men, responds a thoughtful student. Too bad for women, but a good deal for men. But we are thereby deprived of the element of the female critique of male intelligence, the smile at male mastery. Ah, well, is that perhaps why near the end Sophie smiles sweetly at Robert, saying "I can't walk on water"?

The search for telos or intentionality involves an explanation of conclusions, that of the theorists, the films and the students' analyses of both. Most students see conclusions as codas, bits tacked on like the tails of dogs. So they need to learn to focus on final goals. "Slumdog Millionaire" also works well in this regard. The Bollywood dance on the station platform seems to be just that: Bollywood, Hollywood hoopla. But is it just that? Why so many people dancing instead of just the two lovers? Why do they all do the same dance? Why are the others celebrating Slumdog's victory? And what about the deaths of loved ones and the scars on the survivors?

Chapter Four: Jacques Lacan and post-Freudianism

The best students realize that Lacan's writings are difficult, not only because of the ideas, but also because the intended audience seems to be a sort of in-group or coterie. To explain this "encrypting" process, to use a Derridean term, I point out that in questioning orthodox Freudians, Lacan is not merely presenting new conceptions but threatening the very livelihood of practicing psychoanalysts, a field that even in the mid-20th century brought rich financial rewards and great prestige, particularly in Europe. So Lacan was seen as a great threat and cocooned himself with his followers in an occult language. In short, he was threatening the livelihood of his colleagues in the profession. Moreover, most of what we read of Lacan was not originally intended as a publication but was formed from notes from seminars to aid his followers and students.

I begin teaching the texts by going back to Saussure and the Structuralists because the mirror stage derives from their linguistic position. The point to stress about this background material is their insistence that language is not a tool that one learns to wield like a hammer or pliers. Rather, it is a system. Here I use the analogy of a game. Language for Lacan is similar to sports like baseball or cricket. You would not assume that having the bat and ball and being familiar with the rules would enable you to play the game. So too with language: vocabulary and grammar rules are not sufficient to speak a foreign language. Why? You need to play the game with others, that is, to speak with those who know the language, because the vocabulary and rules are not logical or referential in an obvious way. We say "the door"; the French say "la porte." Yet we say portal for doorway: no logical explanation can be offered. But if a Frenchman pointed to a door and called it a "porte," we would think he was at sea, which he probably is, poor devil. Saussure demonstrated that language is not a simple substitution of word for thing. Swift satirized this view by having one of his projectors in *Gulliver's Travels* recommend that instead of speaking we should carry objects with us and point to them, thereby avoiding misunderstanding. The absurdity of this idea makes clear that language is not referential in a simple fashion but much more complex. Here Lacan's anecdote of the two children coming into the railway station makes the same point.

Once language is understood as a system or game with consistent but arbitrary rules, we can proceed to Lacanian psychology. Language does refer beyond itself to what is called "reality," but Lacan insists this is an ideal that is never realized, that is, we who share a culture believe in a "reality" that in another culture may be seen as sheer fantasy. In any event, the move from language to "reality," to the signified, requires interpretation which is often buried or tacit, as in the expression "the sun rises," referring, in literal terms, to "the earth turns." The mirror stage involves the self or ego being immersed in a linguistic system from the moment we associate our image with our given name. From that point onward we are part of a discursive system which, like writing or speaking, permits some individual expression but only within clear parameters and rules, that is, grammar, spelling, pronunciation, conventions of politeness, etc. Lacan asserts that to conceive of the ego in terms of instincts or drives apart from language is misleading and counterproductive. Language is always there from the outset and is the only means at the disposal of the psychoanalyst—and it is important to make clear that Lacan was not a philosopher but a practicing psychoanalyst.

Finally, I find that many students are resistant to the notion that their identity is wholly present in language. Many believe that they have a core ego prior to learning to speak, and they may be right. For our purposes, this debate is more fruitfully left to psychologists and psychoanalysts for whom this matter is still hotly contested. Whether the ego is wholly or in part a product of discourse, Lacan shows us that we need to be aware of its effect upon us. Any of the films in this chapter demonstrate that point quite emphatically: any character in these films who neglects language or the psychological ramifications of language pays a heavy price. Now I turn directly to Lacan's great innovation, the unconscious as language, a notion that also will probably meet with some resistance. Again, I would take evasive action: even if language is only secondary, it is the only means we have of access to the unconscious, so the psychoanalyst follows a procedure like that of a literary critic, listening or reading in order to understand what the speaker or writer is trying to communicate. The difference is that the psychoanalyst looks for what is hidden or masked and the literary critic remains with the text. But they both use the same means toward a different end, because all of us are to some extent like literary characters involved in discourse, a context that requires interpretation. What all of the films show is the danger of proceeding as if language were referential, clear glass, rather than opaque glass presenting a "reality" glimpsed only by way of decoding. From the Queen's dismissal of "the people's princess" as ephemeral journalism to the King's assumption that his speech impediment is merely mechanical, we see the necessity of interpretation, not only for us if we are to understand the movies, but also for the subjects involved in order to resolve their problems. Lacan's psychoanalytic method pertains to the act of interpretation in both a literary and extra-literary context.

Chapter Five: Post-Marxism, Fredric Jameson

I begin teaching post-Marxism by tackling the problem of what is dialectics, a term most students do not understand. My explanation is by way of an analogy with magnetism, appropriate since in Hegel's and Marx's time electromagnetism was a major scientific concern. Two contradictory poles set up a field different from either in isolation, and the result is that neither pole predominates. Instead, their interaction produces something quite different than could be predicted from their individual properties. Of course, the difference between magnetism and dialectics is that the latter is stable while the former, for Hegel, may change and for Marx will inevitably change. Hegel's dialectic involves the rise of individual self-consciousness, an ascent that is not necessary and that may be stalled at any stage. Hegel is usually categorized as an idealist, the dialectical procedure is designed to rise to what he called "Absolute Spirit." Marx's dialectic is history itself that is subject by definition to change, and so the destabilization and movement of the dialectic is not a matter of individual self-consciousness. In fact, Marx asserted that the material world, that is history, changed first and that self-consciousness then followed. Jameson tries to combine both, preserving a place for individual self-consciousness within Marx's historical dialectic. The inner form of literature, Jameson's innovation, is really the voice of the self-conscious individual which Jameson believes has been ignored or drowned out by vulgar Marxism that focuses only upon larger historical forces beyond the control of any single person. Jameson's interest in the single self-conscious voice—and it is important that it is the self-conscious voice in that the person knowingly or consciously is putting forward, not necessarily him or herself, but his or her personal position. This deliberate putting forward of one's own position in the arts involves for Jameson the intermingling of form and content; art works on us in strange and wondrous ways by virtue of this combination.

Any of the films will provide vivid examples: "Il Postino," my personal favorite, uses music to give a formal structure to the Mario–Neruda relationship so that at the end, when Neruda imagines Mario's death, the musical motif of the accordion returns now as a "soft-pedaled" piano. In this way, the movie speaks to us, saying that Mario has finally joined Neruda, not just as a friend or a budding poet, but as an artist whose poetry has an effect on history. And here we can see why Jameson as a post-Marxist is particularly interested in art and insistent that its voice must be included within the historical dialectic. Artists at their best have original ideas and present them in forms that speak beautifully and articulately to us. So, for Jameson, to ignore that source of innovative ideas, ideas that are successfully communicated to others, is a great loss to the Marxist, for it is a source of new possibilities for the future, a factor that could influence positive change, a force of history. Finally, since many assume that Marxism is synonymous with revolution, the students need to be assured that not all Marxists believe that change must involve violent upheavals. On the contrary, a post-Marxist like Jameson implies that art often provides a means of peacefully and lawfully subverting and changing the establishment. But be warned, orthodox or what Jameson calls "vulgar Marxists" will regard this idea as a "cop-out," what Marx called "bourgeois propaganda," that is, the middle-class establishment seeming to tolerate the subversive artist but not really changing its fundamental principles. That is why Jameson argues that his version of Marxism must incorporate Hegel's self-conscious individual voice, which is quintessentially that of the artist.

Chapter Six: Post-feminism: Hélène Cixous

In teaching Cixous's work as an instance of feminism or feminine theory, I emphasize two concepts: process rather than product; and the intermingling of the critical and the creative.

Cixous's version of feminism is that all male master narratives, all-encompassing ideas, are subject to deconstruction. But while Derrida advocates deconstruction for any purpose, Cixous implies that the goal should be concrete and specific, the elucidation of a work of art and/or the advancement of a cause, be it social, political, or philosophical. For this reason libido, the sex drive that precedes but may not necessarily move on to love, is the moving force of this process. You must care deeply about the matter and should make that care overt. Yes, like Derrida, you may play with the language and should be playful about yourself, not take yourself too seriously, but the issue is serious. You always know what Cixous cares about; often with Derrida it is hard to tell. Sometimes for Derrida it seems to be the sheer joy of philosophical play. There are worse things you can do with your time, but Cixous seldom allows herself this luxury. As a feminist, she is constantly confronted with injustice, not only to women but also to minorities, individuals, and innovative ideas. The results of such a process theory are provisional conclusions, momentary goals that serve a specific purpose but are subject to revision by fresh projects, new needs, by history. In that sense, the process is unending; mastery is an illusion. But along the way, works of art are illuminated and problems are resolved or, for a time, remedied. Like a good gerontologist, the Cixousian theorist cannot alter the aging process, that is, history, but can soothe and lengthen the path by focusing upon particularly vexing problems. While Derrida "problematizes" issues of interest to him, Cixous attends to issues evoked by care for others, the ultimate force of libido.

The intermingling of creative and critical is difficult for students since they are usually clearly separated. So they assume that a work is either predominantly creative or critical and theoretical, an old binarism that is difficult to give up. But, of course, Cixous is both at once. Nor is she trying in some underhanded way to foist her theories on innocent readers of her literature or vice versa, surreptitiously presenting her literature as theory.

Rather, her way of thinking pervades all aspects of her work, as it does for most of us, although few of us can do either as well as she does both. I encourage the students to read her creative work as they would any story or play, and analyze it accordingly. Then and only then should they relate it to her critical writing. But the two are related for Cixous—and here is another difference between her work and that of Derrida—because all of her writings are, like literature, teleological, that is, with specific end goals and thus amenable to the hermeneutics of interpretation.

Finally, I encourage the students not to dismiss provisional conclusions as a mere patching up or band-aid, for they well know from their frequent visits to computer stores that complete systems are, in our fast-changing times, past their shelf life as soon as they hit the market. I use "Rosenstrasse" to illustrate all of these points. Most importantly, the conclusion is decidedly provisional. What will happen to these Jewish men ultimately is open to question, but that does not take away one iota from the accomplishment of the women. They have preserved some days of togetherness between themselves and their husbands that will undoubtedly be cherished, and if only one man escapes from the death camps, that alone will make it all worthwhile. Moreover, this provisional goal is most clearly motivated by love of their husbands, something so obvious that it alone must have been so apparent as to stop the soldiers from firing their guns at them. And the accomplishment of the women is completely feminine in that not a single aggressive act was committed by them, and, in fact, that is how and why they won at least a temporary victory. And if their victory is only in having postponed the inevitable, put off for a few days or weeks the time when their men will be taken away, let anyone ask a survivor of the Holocaust if a day less of that hell was worth struggling to attain.

Conclusion

At the end of the class, students often ask what is my theory, by which they mean, my master theory. I send them to my book, listed in the Bibliography below, for my position, not, I believe, a master theory. But I conclude by warning them about the opiate of theory, the belief that a comprehensive notion is in itself superior to an eclectic mixture. Usually world events provide illustrations. For example, at the time of writing the West and many other parts of the world are gripped by a financial crisis. The sole solution posed is an economic theory. And it is important to understand that the seemingly simple pocket theory is a theory, namely that countries like individuals cannot continue to pay out money when their pockets are empty. The analogy between people and countries is highly abstract and, in my view, a very questionable theory. This theory is causing mass protests throughout the world because some people, many close to the source, if not the cause, of the problem are only slightly affected while those losing homes and jobs had little if anything to do with causing the problem. If we are to avoid a world cataclysm, this theory will have to be modified by an alternative one more concerned with the ethics of responsibility than balance sheets. That process is presently being fought out in Brussels among European politicians. Only one thing is certain to me. No single theory can or will prevail. Do not dismiss eclecticism. It may save our world.

BIBLIOGRAPHY

Preface

Ralph Cohen. "Literary Theory as a Genre," in *Centrum* (Spring, 1975).

Northrop Frye. *Anatomy of Criticism*, Princeton: Princeton University Press, 1957.

Rene Wellek and Austin Warren. *Theory of Literature*, New York: Harcourt Brace and Co., 1949.

Chapter One

Jacques Derrida. "Structure, Sign, and Play in the Discourse of the Human Sciences," in *The Structuralist Controversy*, Richard Macksey and Eugenio Donato (eds), Baltimore, Maryland: The Johns Hopkins University Press, 1970.

—*Of Grammatology*, Baltimore, Maryland: The Johns Hopkins University Press, 1998 (first published in French in 1967 as *De la Grammatologie*).

—*Margins of Philosophy*, trans. Alan Bass, Chicago: University of Chicago Press, 1982 (first published in French in 1972 as *Marges de la Philosophie*).

—"White Mythology; Metaphor in the Text of Philosophy," in *New Literary History*, 6 (Autumn, 1974).

Chapter Two

Michel Foucault. "What is an Author," *Language, Counter-Memory, Practice*, Donald F. Bouchard (ed.), Ithaca, NY: Cornell University Press, 1977.

—"The Discourse on Language," in *Social Science Information* (10). London: Sage Publications, 1971.

—*The History of Sexuality*, vol. I, London: Penguin Books, 1978.

—*Beyond Structuralism and Hermeneutics*, Hubert L. Dreyfus and Paul Rabinow (eds), Chicago: University of Chicago Press, 1983.

—*Discipline and Punish. The Birth of the Prison*, New York: Vintage Books, 1995.

Chapter Three

Wolfgang Iser. "The Reading Process: A Phenomenological Approach," in *New Literary History*, 3 (1972).
—*How To Do Theory*. Oxford: Blackwell, 2006.
—*The Fictive and the Imaginary: Charting Literary Anthropology*. Baltimore: The Johns Hopkins University Press, 1993.
—"Towards a Literary Anthropology," in Ralph Cohen (ed.), *The Future of Literary Theory*, London: Routledge, 1989.

Chapter Four

Jacques Lacan. *Ecrits: A Selection*, London: Routledge, 1989.

Chapter Five

Michael Hardt and Kathi Weeks (eds). *The Jameson Reader*, Oxford: Blackwell Publishers, 2000.
Fredric Jameson. *Marxism and Form*, Princeton, NJ: Princeton University Press, 1971.

Chapter Six

Hélène Cixous. "The Laugh of Medusa," in *Signs*, 1 (Summer, 1976).
Marta Segarra (ed.). *The Portable Cixous*, New York: Columbia University Press, 2010.
Susan Sellers (ed.). *The Hélène Cixous Reader*, London: Routledge, 1994.

Conclusion

Michael Hardt and Kathi Weeks (eds). *The Jameson Reader*, Oxford: Blackwell Publishers, 2000.
Edward Tomarken. *Genre and Ethics, The Education of an Eighteenth Century Critic*, London: Associated University Press, 2002.

INDEX